THE STAMPED AND STENCILED HOME

THE STAMPED
AND STENCILED HOME

Easy, beautiful designs for walls, floors, and home accessories

DORIS GLOVIER

ROCKPORT PUBLISHERS

First published in the United States of America by
Rockport Publishers, Inc.
33 Commercial Street
Gloucester, Massachusetts 01930-5089
Telephone: (978) 282-9590
Fax: (978) 283-2742
www.rockpub.com

Library of Congress Cataloging-in-Publication Data
Glovier, Doris Cast.
   The stamped and stenciled home : easy, beautiful designs for walls,
floors, and home accessories / Doris Cast Glovier.
      p.   cm.
   ISBN 1-56496-897-9
   1. Stencil work. I. Title.
TT270 .G59 2002
745.7'3—dc21   2002004521

ISBN 1-56496-897-9

10 9 8 7 6 5 4 3 2 1

Design: Peter King & Company
Cover Image: Bobbie Bush Photography www.bobbiebush.com
Special thanks to Hanna Wingate of Rockport, Massachusetts
Photographer: Bobbie Bush Photography www.bobbiebush.com
Copy Editor: Pamela Hunt
Proofreader: Pamela Angulo
Project Designer: Doris Glovier

Printed in China
Printed in Hong Kong
Printed in Singapore

Photographer: Brian Vanden Brink

CONTENTS

OPPOSITE This patio table is set with linens and accessories which are whimsical and charming. The line drawn style of the motifs applied to the simple white of the tablecloth adds artistry and imagination to the simple patio set. Basic white napkins and place mats repeat selected elements of the design. Painting on glass is no longer a problem, as illustrated by the decorated pitcher and glass set. The festive colors in the design recur in the flowers that are arranged in the stenciled birdhouse planter. Photo provided courtesy of Delta Technical Coatings.

INTRODUCTION

Have you ever looked around your home and felt uninspired by the environment? Do you dream of customizing it to reflect your personal style? Have you ever come home after an evening at a friend's home and felt that your home, in comparison, needed updating?

The Stamped and Stenciled Home introduces new ideas and ways to make your home a reflection of your unique style. The color palettes featured in this book demonstrate how to achieve your chosen effect, be it contemporary, cool and sophisticated, fun and funky, or warm and traditional. The projects provide inspiration beyond mere wall borders and repeating patterns; you'll be able to create beautiful, memorable rooms that speak of inventive grandeur or innovative, imaginative joy. Open your mind as you open this book and experience true creativity. Envision your own personalized space that speaks to you and to everyone and proclaims, "I am exceptional!"

ABOVE This brilliant blue wall is all the more dramatic when embellished with the simple gold star motif. The simplicity creates a subtle, sophisticated impact. Gold star shapes actually seem to radiate light from the deep shade of blue on the wall. This room requires little in the way of furnishings to leave an impression upon the visitor. Photographer: Bick/Freundin

OPPOSITE This living area has a traditional feel, but the addition of the stylized pine branches gives it a fresh twist. The soft shade of yellow on the walls combines with the natural wood tones to create a warm glow within the space. Photographer: Brian Vanden Brink/James Beyor, Builder

For the purpose of safety and ease of use, only products that require soap and water for cleanup are used to create the projects in this book.

CHAPTER 1

THE BASICS OF STAMPING AND STENCILING

Decorating with paint is the simplest and least expensive way to dramatically change the personality of a space. From faux finishing to stenciling and stamping, transforming a room with various painting techniques just makes good sense. An impressive makeover can be accomplished in less than a day, smaller projects in just a few hours. Decorating with paint is more than easy and inexpensive; it's fun as well!

OPPOSITE The purple blooms of these stenciled hydrangeas coordinate nicely with the cool lavender walls of the room. Crisp white-painted woodwork and sheer curtains create a striking ensemble for the stenciled blossoms. Serenity prevails in this space while lovely motifs dance upon the white panels on the wall and surrounding the windows. Photo courtesy of Plaid Enterprises, Inc.

GENERAL POINTERS

Get organized. Prepare your work area. Gather all of the supplies for your project. You'll need to organize all of your supplies—stencils, stamps, tools, and paints—so that you will have easy access to them. If you will be using a ladder, don't forget to place a drop cloth beneath it.

Make sure that your work surface is clean and dry. When stenciling or stamping on walls, use a basecoat of latex paint with a flat, satin, or eggshell finish. Keep in mind that the paints that have been suggested for these projects will not adhere as well to walls or other surfaces that have a high gloss finish. Your paint dealer can suggest ways to prepare furniture or walls to accept water-based paints.

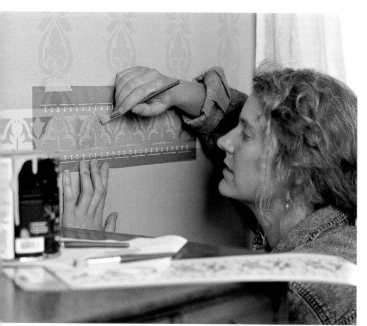

Photo courtesy of American Traditional Stencils.

STENCILING — TOOLS & MATERIAL

A list of the materials you will need for stenciling follows.

Stencil Brushes

Use good-quality brushes made specifically for stenciling. You need several brushes, at least one for each color that you use. Keep in mind that a small design requires a small brush, a large design a larger brush. You will rarely need the largest brush sizes available, unless you are creating a very large design. Purchase soft-bristled brushes. Stiff-bristled brushes are useful for heavy, textured fabrics like canvas. Always remember to begin stenciling with a dry brush.

Sponges

The small crafting sponges on the market today are quite wonderful. Some are triangular and some are square. Many people use the small craft sponge to stencil, but purists use only a stencil brush. Why not try both? For long, repetitive borders, the sponge allows you to stencil much faster, and cleanup is a breeze. Because the brush offers more control, a certain amount of artistry may be lost with the sponge—consider it a better opportunity for artistic quality.

Stencil Paints

• Acrylic craft paints are water-based, which means that cleanup can be accomplished with only soap and water. They are easy to find and inexpensive. Acrylic paints are a bit more vivid than some other types of paint, and you can mix two or more colors together to create custom colors. They tend to dry quickly, so you may want to add extender to your paint to increase the open time (how long the paint remains moist and workable) and transparency. Follow the manufacturer's directions for use.

• Stencil gels are readily available and easy to use. Because they are available in small quantities, the cost can be minimal. Like acrylic paints, stencil gels can be cleaned up with soap and water.

- Stencil creams offer an alternative to paints and gels. They come in a solid state, so you don't need to be concerned about spillage. The stenciled effect is soft and a bit more translucent than designs created with acrylic paints. However, because creams often contain oil, the drying time is a bit longer. A spray all-purpose sealer can be applied to speed up the drying time. Cleanup of stencil creams requires soap and warm water.

- Stencil crayons are another option for stenciling. The texture is similar to the stencil creams. Follow the manufacturer's directions for use.

- Fabric paints are washable and work well on many fabrics. You can usually clean up fabric paint with soap and water.

Stencils

- Single-layer stencils are simple designs that have "bridges" or breaks between colors. They are the least expensive, but they offer the least amount of detail. Most of the designs in the Patterns and Templates section are single-layer designs.

- Multiple-layer stencils have greater detail and fewer bridges or breaks in the design than single-layer stencils. The additional detail in multiple-layer stencils provides more opportunity for artistic work.

- Theorem stencils always have multiple layers. A finished theorem stencil design has absolutely no bridges or breaks in the motif.

- Handcut stencils can be created from acetate or plastic. Just select your design or motif and cut it out with a craft knife or stencil burner. You can purchase the stencil burner at your craft or art store, but be careful when using it because these heated cutters are extremely hot. The best way to cut a stencil is to place your pattern under tempered glass (such as the glass from an old picture frame) and tape it into position. Tape the stencil

material to the top side of the glass and cut out your design. Do not use a stencil burner if you create your hand-cut stencils in this way. Be sure to leave at least a 1" (3 cm) border or margin around your design. Another material that you can use for a stencil is poster board. Just use a sharp craft knife to cut out your design. The main disadvantage to using poster board is that you cannot see through it to place the stencil precisely where you want it.

Other General Supplies

- Masking tape, easy-release painter's tape, or repositionable stencil spray adhesive is necessary to hold your stencil in place.

- A pencil is useful to indicate the location of your stencil's registration marks.

- A chalk line comes in handy when marking or aligning horizontal or vertical designs.

- Ladders and paper towels may be necessary.

- Brush cleaner will be needed. However, for stencil brushes, I prefer to use the leading grease-dissolving dishwashing liquid.

- A commercial palette or palette pad is necessary for arranging your acrylic paints. A white Styrofoam or grease-resistant paper plate also works well.

- A stencil mask, which protects an area that is not to be painted, is very useful when creating complex designs. Create a mask from an old greeting card or excess stencil material. It is handy to have several masks in different shapes, such as rectangles, curves, V-shaped cutouts, and other configurations. Just place the mask over the area of the stencil that you want to protect.

- Tracing paper is useful when copying patterns and designing stencils.

STENCILING TECHNIQUES

The secret to good stenciling is to use a small amount of high-quality paint and stencil brushes that are not too stiff. Stenciling is more of a shading process than a painting technique. You need a clean, dry brush for each color. Remember to use a small brush for small areas and shading. Use a medium-sized brush for other areas. Use registration marks to help you line up the stencil, or just eyeball it for accuracy. Create a few practice stencils to get the hang of it before starting your project.

Basic Stenciling Procedure

1. Use masking tape, painter's tape, or spray adhesive to affix the stencil to your project.

2. Squeeze out a small amount of gel or acrylic paint onto a palette and dip the brush lightly into the paint. If you are using stencil creams, scrape off the top layer of paint to get to the usable paint below. Swirl your brush in the paint in the container.

3. It is critical to remove almost all of the paint from your brush to make a clean design. Firmly swirl the brush onto a folded paper towel. To make sure that you have removed enough paint from your brush, swirl a stroke on an edge of your stencil. If the paint smears, you still have too much paint on the brush.

4. Swirl the brush in small circular motions just inside the cutout area you wish to stencil. Be sure to keep your brush perpendicular to the surface. Artistic stenciling involves light and dark areas and not a solid layer of opaque paint. Where possible, the center of the painted motif should be lighter than the edges. You can achieve this effect by concentrating your swirling around the outer area of the cutouts. Another technique is to pounce the tip of the brush onto the surface. Pouncing does not produce the smooth results of the swirling method, but it is useful in very small cutout areas. If you are using the swirling technique and cannot eliminate the circular brushstrokes, try gently pouncing the area.

5. Shading and shadowing add depth and artistry to a stenciled design. Swirl on a deeper color where shadowing or shading would normally occur. Practice this technique before applying it to your project.

TOP This room feels tropical and fresh with its stenciled lanterns and abundance of flowers. In the corner, stones are piled with plantings adorning the top. The charming wicker furniture features soft pillows stenciled with a number of plants and flowers. This is a handsome example of coordinating room elements and design to complete a custom interior. Photo provided courtesy of Delta Technical Coatings, Inc.

BOTTOM This lovely wall panel depicts a Parisian urn motif embellished by a beautiful Florentine grille border. The elegant artwork is a rich ornamentation for a sophisticated interior. The design, placed low over the table, creates an interesting vignette and is softly illuminated by the glow of the candles. The red walls feature a stenciled Florentine grille pattern. Stencil designer Melanie Royals, Royal Design Studio.

Using Multiple-Layer Stencils

- Artistic stenciling requires the use of multiple colors. Mask off areas you do not want to paint a certain color either with tape or a prepared mask. This process may take a few minutes, but it is time well spent. Accidentally stenciling over an area with the wrong color can be disastrous. Less masking is required with good quality multiple-layer stencils.

- You can use one of two methods for stenciling a repetitive pattern with a multiple-layer stencil. The first method is to begin at point A and stencil only the first layer all the way around the room. Then you begin again at point A with layer two, and stencil all the way around the room. Repeat this process until all of the layers have been stenciled. To save trips up and down the ladder, you can complete each of the layers before moving on to the next repetition. If you are using a slow-drying paint, however, be cautious because smudging can easily occur.

- Registration marks are usually located in the corners of multiple-layer stencils. These tiny cutouts are alignment guides. Place small pieces of tape directly under these marks on your work surface. Make a pencil mark on the tape through each opening so that each piece of tape has a mark on it. When you place the second layer on your work surface, line up the registration openings with the pencil marks to make sure that you have perfect alignment. Continue this process until all overlays have been stenciled. Some stencilists are able to align multiple-layer stencils by eye, but for beginning stencilists, registration marks are a useful tool.

Stenciling Tips

- Always use a dry brush. After you wash your brush, allow it to dry completely before using it again. You should have several stencil brushes, at least one brush for each color that you use.

- You can use artist's brushes to embellish your finished stenciling project with the look of freehand painting. Be sure to purchase good quality brushes — the result is worth it.

- You will need soap and water to clean stencils and brushes. Many brush cleaners are available, and they are probably better for your brushes. Many stencilists use degreasing dishwashing liquid or a leading oil soap for brushes and stencils. Clean them gently. The sooner you clean them, the easier and more effective the job will be. Always use a good-quality brush cleaner for artist's brushes. Follow the manufacturer's directions for use.

STAMPING — TOOLS & MATERIALS

Stamps

Commercially manufactured stamps are available in an array of styles and sizes. Design styles include retro motifs, holidays, and ancient art styles as well as country, contemporary, romance, and cultural themes. They may be fashioned into floral designs, sporting motifs, animals, food, and many other designs. They come mounted on wooden or acrylic blocks, as well as on other materials. You can even find some chunky styles and detailed stamps mounted on a curved base.

You can make handmade stamps from several different materials, such as sponges, potatoes, foam-core board, corrugated paper, and Styrofoam. You can either find these objects around the house or purchase them inexpensively at a craft store. Stamps may be created from thin, flexible sheets of foam purchased at a craft store. Cut the stamp shapes from the soft, dense foam. Glue the shapes to a piece of foam core board that is close to the shape of the stamp pattern. Once the glue is dry, cut the foam core board to the shape of the stamp.

Stamp Pads, Paints, and Ink

- Stamp pads are available pre-inked with a water-based pigment or can be purchased ready to ink. The pre-inked pads are available in single colors or multi-color rainbow pads.

- Inks for stamp pads come in many colors. Fabric inks are permanent and washable.

- You can use embossing ink with embossing powders to create a raised (embossed) effect. A heat tool that is manufactured specifically for this purpose is a necessity for this technique.

- Acrylic paints have become popular in stamping. They are water-based and come in a wide array of colors, as well as in metallic finishes. If you can't find the exact color that you need, you can mix two or more colors together to create custom colors. Acrylic paints are perfect for home decor stamping projects. Most of the projects in this book were created with acrylic paints.

- Fabric paints made for stamping are great to use for their durability. However, the fabric projects in this book were created using acrylic paint with textile medium added.

- Ceramic paints allow you to stamp on glazed surfaces. They are not durable, so hand-wash your finished projects with care.

- Felt-tip markers and pens are invaluable tools in stamping. Use them to color in stamped designs, embellish your work, or add shading to the stamp itself. Embossing pens are used with embossing powders, in the same way that embossing pads are used with embossing powders.

Tools, Supplies, and Equipment

- Brushes, small rollers, and craft sponges may be used to apply paint to the stamp.

- A heat gun is necessary for embossing.

- Measuring tools, a long level, and a chalk line may be necessary to ensure accuracy in the placement of the designs.

- A sharp craft knife and cutting mat or glass are used for cutting out the stencils.

- You will need a sturdy ladder and drop cloth for most wall work.

STAMPING TECHNIQUES

There are two ways to apply color to a stamp. If you are using a stamp pad, tap the stamp on the stamp pad several times, making sure that the raised areas of the rubber image are covered with ink. If you are using paint, apply the paint with a craft sponge or brush to the raised edges of the rubber image. Do not overload the stamp with ink or paint. All of the stamping projects in this book were created with acrylic paints.

- Be sure to practice stamping your design on a separate surface that is similar to the project surface to eliminate any undesirable results.

- To apply a stamped impression, press the stamp onto the surface using even pressure, and then lift straight up. Do not attempt to make a better impression by rocking the stamp on the surface. Continue stamping if you desire multiple impressions, reloading the stamp with paint or ink as needed. If the stamp's design is detailed, you will need to use less paint or ink.

- You can embellish the stamped image with colored pencils or pens.

- Let your project dry completely, especially before stamping in another color.

- When you are finished or between colors, begin to clean the stamp by repeatedly stamping it onto a paper towel until most of the color is gone. Then wash the stamp immediately with mild dishwashing liquid and warm water.

Handmade Stamps

If you can ink or apply paint to a material or an object, then you can use it as a stamp. For home decor, the quality of the stamped image is important, so make sure to use materials that create crisp, consistent images.

Dense craft foam is an excellent material for handmade stamps. You can purchase square thin sheets of this flexible, soft product in craft stores. You can easily and cleanly cut out shapes with a sharp craft knife. Just cut out your shapes and glue them onto your backing.

Foam-core board makes an excellent backing. Adding a block or handle is not always necessary, but it does make the stamping process a bit easier and less messy. The backing should be no larger than the stamp and, if made with a hard material, should have a cushion between the stamp and the block.

OPPOSITE The open window creates the impression that these stenciled apple tree branches have simply extended their fragrant blossoms indoors. The live plants and vintage birdhouse are charming additions to the nature theme. These embellishments add warmth and charm to this dining area. Photo courtesy of Plaid Enterprises, Inc.

GENERAL INFORMATION

ENLARGING A PATTERN

You will need to enlarge the images in the Patterns and Templates chapter to match the sizes of the patterns used in the sample projects. Design instructions include the finished design size. There are several ways to enlarge a pattern. You can photocopy the design right out of the book, using the copy machine to enlarge the image by the percentage recommended in the pattern section. You can also take the book to your local copy store and ask their employees to enlarge your pattern to the desired size. You can also trace the design, cut out the tracing, and measure it. Scan the traced design, and open the scanned file in a graphics program. From the graphics program, you should be able to print the image at the desired size. Remember that the designs provided are for your personal use. They are protected under copyright laws and are not to be reproduced for marketing purposes.

INTERESTING AND EASY WALL FINISHES

Today's interiors have walls with personality. Walls with a vivid color or a dramatic faux finish provide a much more interesting background for stencils and stamping than plain white walls. Neutral wall glaze is often required in faux finishing. It is a colorless, thick liquid that can be mixed with latex or acrylic paint. The glaze mixture is generally applied over a basecoated wall of eggshell or satin latex paint. Only water-based products are suggested for the projects in the book. Work with a partner when creating a faux finish, with one person applying the paint or glaze while the other works it. Make sure to purchase the best available neutral wall glaze. Glazes with longer open times ensure that the glaze will stay wet longer, allowing you to work it longer. For finishes such as frottage or color washing, a longer open time is essential for good results.

ABOVE The contemporary style of furniture in this arrangement is the perfect offset for the early-style stenciled border pattern. The mustard gold walls create a bold background for the painted design.
Photographer: Bick/Freundin

Latex paint with an eggshell or satin finish is the best base for the finishes described here. The glaze mixture should always be a shade or two lighter or darker than the basecoat for the best effect.

When working with wall finishes requiring a glaze mixture, always do a sample board first to test your color and technique. Working with glazes is very different from working with paint. If you will be painting a basecoat on your wall before creating the faux finish, you should practice your faux finish technique on the old painted surface first—you'll be painting over it, anyway. This practice takes a little extra time, but it ensures that you achieve the results that you want. Keep in mind that the results on the new painted surface may differ slightly.

Sponging

Sponging, the simplest of all wall finishes, gives a lovely, textural appearance to your surface. For the best results, use three colors—a basecoat and two additional colors that are closely related in color to the basecoat. Colors that vary greatly sometimes result in a splotchy appearance. After applying a latex basecoat, mix latex or acrylic paint with the neutral wall glaze. Use the ratio recommended by the manufacturer or the project instructions. Dampen a natural sea sponge with water, squeeze out the excess water and blot on a dry towel. Dip the sponge in the glaze mixture and blot it on a paper towel. As you sponge the wall, turn the sponge as you work. If you are going to use another color, space your sponging accordingly. Be sure not to overlap the color. Use a small piece of sponge for corners and small areas. After the paint has dried, apply the other color.

Color Wash

A color wash finish is achieved by applying one or two thin coats of color over a basecoat. The shades that you use should be close in color. The translucent effect gives the wall a soft, watercolored appearance or an aged look, depending upon the colors you use. You can make a color wash by diluting latex paint with water or with glaze. Apply the color wash with a brush in a wide, crosshatching motion, beginning in the corner of the room and covering a four-foot square area. The more you work the brush, the softer the look. For an even softer appearance, brush over the area with a dry brush. Work quickly with a partner.

Ragging

There are two types of ragging. The projects in this book use the "ragging on" method. This mottled, lush effect is achieved by applying a paint glaze over a latex basecoat using a rag. Wear gloves to protect your hands for this procedure. Prepare the glaze in a pail according to the manufacturer's directions. Some of the projects in this book list a suggested ratio of paint to glaze. A more translucent effect requires less paint and more glaze. Bunch up a damp, lint-free rag, making sure to form lots of folds and creases. Dip the rag into the pail of glaze mixture, blotting the excess on some paper towels. Begin at the center of the wall and dab the paint on, switching direction to vary the pattern. Continue working, one section at a time, replacing or rinsing out your rag as it becomes full of paint. Take a step back occasionally to see where you may need to add color.

Frottage or Bagging

This beautiful finish creates the look of worn leather and is achieved using plastic sheeting. The glaze finish is applied over a latex basecoat. Prepare a stack of plastic sheets, such as large plastic trash bags that are cut open. Crinkle up the plastic sheets, smooth them out, and place them in a stack close by. Also have a group of small plastic bags crumpled up into wads to use in softening an edge or adding color here and there. Create a mixture of one part glaze to four parts latex or acrylic paint. Working with a partner, roll on a layer of glaze about the size of your larger sheets of plastic. Immediately lay a sheet of plastic over the wet glaze and pat it down with your hands. Then remove the plastic sheet and reveal your beautiful finish. While one person applies and removes the plastic, the other can be applying the next section of paint. Work quickly, never letting the glaze dry. A small wad of plastic makes a great tool in softening any lap lines between sections. Step back occasionally to see if any additional glaze needs to be added.

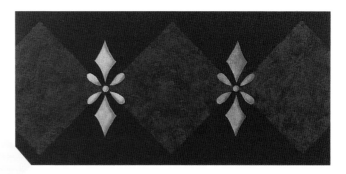

CHAPTER 2

INVITE NATURE INTO YOUR HOME

Life is hectic. From sunup to sundown, our lives are nonstop activity. There never seems to be enough time to experience the beauty of nature, and yet when we do, it brings peace and calm to the spirit. Designing your decor to bring nature indoors can transform a room into a tranquil space to enjoy at the end of a busy day.

This chapter focuses on interior style that evokes natural images. A lovely and light decor can be achieved using the "Ocean Blue" designs.

A rustic and woodsy environment emerges with the application of the "Autumn Leaves" motif. The "Tulips and Starflower" design is so simple, yet creates intimate appeal that converts an uninteresting space into a rich environment. Just use a little imagination, a bit of paint, and some brushes, and any room can be transformed in a matter of hours. Enjoy this collection of beautiful images and creative ideas as you put your own imagination to work.

OPPOSITE TOP RIGHT Fruit and floral themes reside in countless decorative designs throughout history. This stunning rendition of classic style is paired with a taste of the seashore. It also incorporates beautiful vines laden with berries and fruit. The primary decorative motifs in this painted floor are stenciled. Freehand painting is also included. The artwork features a pleasant historic quality fused with an updated style. Artist: Susan Amons. Photographer: Sandy Agrafiotis. Design Firm: Hurlbutt Designs.

OPPOSITE TOP LEFT & BOTTOM Photographer: Brian Vanden Brink/Drysdale Associates Interior Design

THE OCEAN BLUE

Even if you don't live by the sea or own a beach house, this stylish approach to a seaside theme is sophisticated, yet charming. Although the accessories pictured in the room (see the photograph on page 20) indicate that this space could be inhabited by the very young, this theme certainly leaves room to grow. The Ocean Blue project is also a wonderful theme for the living area or den of any home. The subtle shades of color create an atmosphere of perfect serenity. The variation suggestion on page 25 creates the illusion of a soft, ocean-washed background upon which to randomly place the stenciled and stamped motifs. Breathe deeply and you can almost smell the salt air.

SUPPLIES

Starfish stamp, 3¼" (8 cm)
Seashell border stencil, 9½" long (24 cm)
Easy-release painter's tape
Natural sea sponge
Artist's liner brush
Stencil brushes (medium size)
White paint pen (optional)

ACRYLIC PAINT

Yellow ochre
Baby blue
Periwinkle blue
French blue
Soft yellow
White

The starfish motif was created with a handmade stamp. The remaining designs were made with stencils. Prepare or purchase all stencil templates. See Resources, page 124. Templates begin on page 114.

TIP: You can easily achieve a wonderful finish using the sponging technique. You should use at least three colors, the basecoat and two sponged-on colors. The shades should be very close in color to create a subtle look.

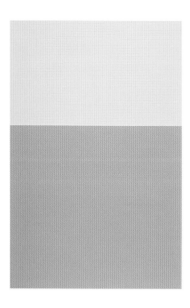

Step 1: Begin by masking off any woodwork and the ceilings with the painter's tape. Always remember to remove the tape as soon as possible to prevent it from removing any of your fresh paint. Paint the walls with a good quality latex paint (with an eggshell or flat finish) in shades of soft yellow and baby blue. Apply the blue paint from the floor or baseboard up the wall 40" (102 cm) or to the chair rail molding. Continue from that point to the ceiling with the yellow paint. Use the painter's tape to mark a line on the wall 7¼" (18 cm) below where the yellow paint begins. This line will help you place the stenciled and painted border. Refer to the photograph for details.

1

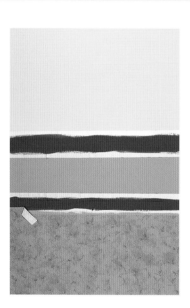

Step 2: Using a slightly damp natural sea sponge, gently sponge the periwinkle blue acrylic paint on the wall below the masked-off border area. The plain band of blue above this sponging is where the stenciled border will go. Continue sponging all around the room below the border area. Sponge over it with French blue, using a light hand to achieve a subtle appearance. After you have created the sponged area, you will paint periwinkle blue stripes to define the stencil border area. Use the painter's tape to mask off a 1¼" (3 cm) stripe at the top of the unsponged band and a ½" (1 cm) stripe along the lower edge. Paint two coats of periwinkle blue and remove tape before the paint dries.

2

Step 3: Stencil the "Ocean Blue" border design within the striped border area. Space the motifs in a pleasing repetition. You can use the starfish template to create either a stencil or a stamp. A handmade stamp was used in the sample project. Stamp or stencil the starfish randomly in the yellow area of the wall. For added drama, outline the motif (refer to photograph for details) to create a three-dimensional effect. To highlight the starfish, use a white paint pen or liner brush with thinned white paint. For the shadowed side, use thinned yellow ochre. To highlight the stencil border, use a white paint pen or liner brush with thinned white paint. To shadow the stencil border, apply a mixture of thinned French blue and a little periwinkle blue with a fine liner brush. This process is optional—it adds a significant amount of time to the project, but it is well worth the effort.

3

OCEAN BLUE VARIATION

You can easily create the illusion of a watery, undulating background using the color wash technique. First apply a soft color wash (one part light aquamarine latex paint to two parts glaze) to white walls, and randomly stamp or stencil the starfish and shell designs in white. Then, follow up with another two-to-one color wash using an ocean blue shade.

ESSENCE OF AUTUMN

This warm and welcoming style works well in a winter lodge or in any room that needs a bit of coziness. The background is a simple and fun sponged technique. The hand-cut border stencil, along with some great stamps from your local craft store or online shop, creates a rich and woodsy atmosphere. No matter the season of the year, your new room decor will warm your spirit.

Medium gold latex wall paint
Neutral wall glaze
Large natural sea sponge
Small craft sponge
Stencil brushes, small and medium
Artist's liner brush
Leaf border stencil, 18" long (46 cm)
Various leaf stamps
    (refer to the Resources, page 124)

ACRYLIC PAINT

Soft yellow
Light golden brown
Terra-cotta
Red iron oxide
Warm brown
Dark green

Prepare or purchase stencils.
See Resources, page 124.

> **TIP.** Acrylic paints can be applied to stamps in several ways. For the best results, use a small dense craft sponge. The wedge-shaped style works extremely well. Enlarge and cut your stencils, or order them (see Resources, page 124) prior to beginning your project. Always practice any procedure before beginning your project. Templates begin on page 114.

Step 1: Make sure that the wall you are working on has a good coat of medium gold latex paint. Remember to mix paint for sponging with one part latex or acrylic paint to two parts glaze, or according to the manufacturer's directions. The sample project was done using acrylic paints. Working with a damp sea sponge, softly pounce on an even layer of soft yellow, slightly deeper than the wall color. Turn the sponge to vary the pattern. As you sponge, the paint will begin to set up a bit. To soften the pattern, pounce the area again without adding more color, twisting the wrist very slightly. This action slightly blurs and softens the sponged color without smearing it. If you do this when the paint is still very wet, you may smear it. Waiting for the paint to begin to set is especially important when you use colors that differ as much as those in the sample project do. The second layer of sponging is of golden oak, and the final layer is of terra-cotta. After all walls are sponged and dry, step back and see if any areas need additional color. If an area is too dark, try sponging on a little of the basecoat color. The color balance is not supposed to be perfectly even, so don't be too critical.

Step 2: Apply the red iron oxide, terra-cotta, dark green, and soft yellow paint to your leaf stamps, and randomly stamp the leaves around the room. Use different color combinations on each stamp to give them richness and realism. The leaves on the sample are placed close together, but you can arrange them in any grouping on your wall. Some leaves should be upside down and sideways to create the appearance of falling leaves. Don't forget to leave room for the stenciled border. You can place it at the top of your wall, at chair rail height, or around doors and windows.

Step 3: When you have completed the stamping, you can begin stenciling the leaf border. Use the same colors that you used for the stamping, with the addition of a deep brown for the branches. Stencil on the leaves, making sure to use a mask over any areas to which you do not want to apply the color you are using. Concentrate the colors on the edges of the leaves. As you can see in the sample, all of the colors are randomly applied, but the dark forest shade is dominant. Stencil in the warm brown branches. Continue stenciling until all areas are complete. If desired, use a artist's liner brush and the warm brown paint to add veins to the centers of the leaves. Be sure to dilute the paint to an ink consistency so that you can paint a thin line. See the photograph for details.

SUMMER LEAF DESIGN VARIATION

This variation of the leaf design creates a light and airy atmosphere. The contemporary edge is quite different from the deep, rich feel of the Essence of Autumn design. The simple variation is done on a soft yellow background. An apple green color is all that is needed to stamp on these attractive images. Include a dragonfly stamp for added interest.

TULIPS AND STARFLOWERS

The simplicity and elegance of tulips and starflowers can lend a sense of quiet and tranquility to your room. You can stencil this design in a repetitive vertical pattern to create a charming wallpapered look. This beautiful motif is striking in its simplicity. Some time is involved because of the overall stenciling pattern, but no color changes are necessary. Begin by preparing the room for painting. The featured sample was created using a soft moss green latex basecoat. An alternative to the repetitive pattern is to apply the sprigs randomly about the room for a springy, fanciful look.

SUPPLIES

Soft moss green latex wall paint
Chalk
Stencil brushes, small and medium
Tulip and Starflower stencil, 15" long (38 cm)
Small craft sponge

STENCIL CREAM PAINT

White

Enlarge and cut out your stencils, or order them prior to beginning your project. If you are cutting your own stencil, it will save time during the stenciling to place three repeats (stems) on the stencil. This means that as you stencil, one of the stems can be lined up over the last painted stem. Study the project photographs before cutting your stencil. Please note that the stem direction can be reversed with each repeat. Templates begin on page 114. The stem motif for the project is 15" (38 cm) long. This pattern includes two stems.

TIP: Stencil creams generally take a bit longer to dry than acrylic paints or stencil gels. Be careful not to smear the cream as you go along. Aerosol spray is available at craft stores to set the paint immediately.

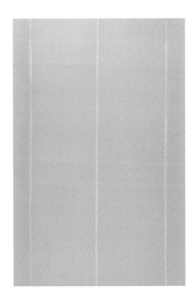

Step 1: Begin by masking off any woodwork and the ceiling with painter's tape. Paint two coats of a soft moss green latex paint on your walls. Let it dry thoroughly. Plan your vertical floral patterns, and draw the pattern on the walls in chalk, allowing for starting and stopping points in the corners. You don't have to make your marks as heavy as those in the photograph. Those lines are bold for easy viewing. Only an intermittent dash is necessary on the wall. Use a retractable tape measure and a long level when drawing the lines to ensure that they are straight. You can also make a plumb bob by attaching a small weight to the end of a string. Marking off your walls at ceiling height, tape the string to the mark, and carefully make intermittent marks down the wall along the string. Check your marks with a long level. As you near a corner, adjust the vertical lines to ensure that the final stenciled line does not straddle a door molding or a corner angle.

Step 2: Tape your stencil to the wall where you intend to begin stenciling. If you are using stencil cream, you will need to scrape off the protective top layer of the paint. Swirl your stencil brush in the paint and offload most of the paint by firmly swirling it on a paper towel. Begin stenciling the design, moving from the bottom of the wall to the top. The second vertical line of motifs will begin in the middle of the branch to stagger the design. Refer to the photograph for details. Continue stenciling around the room until all of the walls are complete. Remove any chalk residue with a dry stencil brush.

TIP: Using a color chart to choose colors makes good sense. When combining shades in a room, a color wheel or chart takes the worry out of whether the colors will work together.

TULIP AND STARFLOWER VIBRANT PINK AND APPLE GREEN VARIATION

To create this fun and funky alternative, mark off seven-inch intervals at the top of the wall. Use a level to make your lines down the wall at these 7" (18 cm) intervals. Center your ¾" (2 cm) painter's tape over these lines to indicate where the thin, white stripes will be. With a large sea sponge, pounce the pink paint on every other stripe. Sponge the apple green paint on the remaining stripes. Remove the tape as you go, revealing your white stripe. After the pink and apple green paint has dried, randomly stencil the flower stems and starflower blooms in white paint on the painted stripes.

TULIP AND STARFLOWER VARIATION

This charming combination begins with walls painted with white latex paint. The flower stems are used individually to brighten up a dreary space. Before stenciling, mark the walls with small pieces of tape where you intend to place a stem. Be sure to leave space between the stems to add a stenciled or stamped starflower bloom. The colors used in this project were soft medium green, bright yellow, deep lilac, and rich pink.

"THE OCEAN BLUE" STOOL

This charming wooden stool with its nautical flavor creates a perfect resting spot for those weary feet. Why not use it near a sunny window as a plant stand where the sun and a gentle breeze softly reign? The vivid style makes the piece a fun addition to your seaside decor. Complete this project using the colors listed and the patterns featured in the template section on page 114. The sponged finish is detailed in the project instructions. Tape off the areas on the legs and top to apply stripes using the suggested color palette. Protect your finished stool by applying a water-based sealer or varnish.

TIP: Before attempting any painting or crafting process, always practice on a similar surface first. This will assure you of a finished project with pleasing results. You should keep the basecoat color available when creating projects like this in case you need to apply a quick layer over mistakes. Remember, if you make a mistake, just paint over it and start again.

Photographer: Bobbie Bush

SUMMER LEAF CURTAINS

You can purchase a set of lined, white curtains inexpensively at most department stores. Wash and iron the curtains first, and then apply stamped designs in apple green or the color of your choice. Be sure to mix textile medium into your acrylic paint, according to the manufacturer's directions. Let this project inspire you to turn an inexpensive set of curtains into a coordinating accessory.

TULIP AND STARFLOWER PILLOWS

If you sew, the pillow style shown will be a simple project. Stencil or stamp the design after the front panel of the pillow is cut. To stencil or stamp the design on a finished pillow, carefully snip the seam stitches to access the pillow stuffing. Remove the stuffing and insert a piece of rigid cardboard larger than the design area and place it on a flat surface. Stencil or stamp the design on the fabric. If you use acrylic paints, add textile medium for durability. Replace the stuffing, and stitch up the opening.

T I P: Although certain types of stencil paints are mentioned in this book, use what you already have. From stencil creams to acrylic paint and stencil gels, the unique properties of each medium offer quite different results. Experiment with each type of paint to see what you prefer, but by all means, if you have something already available at home, use it.

CHAPTER 3

SIMPLE AND SOPHISTICATED

Sophisticated interior design suggests majesty without the hindrance of extravagant clutter. The decor of many contemporary homes today speaks of the need to simplify our world. Sophisticated decor can have many faces. Opulence and excessiveness certainly resonate of the refined and sophisticated style that we associate with the past. However, the desire to simplify a complex existence is the impetus behind much of today's decor. What an exquisite pleasure it is to close the door on the chaotic business of the day and experience the tranquility of order and beauty. The projects in this chapter reflect traditional design with contemporary clean lines.

OPPOSITE LEFT The sophisticated shades of gold, which are warmed by the sun from the sheer-draped window near the rocking chair, create a cozy glow. The repeated pattern results in a pleasing effect using this tone-on-tone color palette. A horizontal border is also stenciled and is a lovely pattern that complements its companion design. A tall, ornate mantle is topped with a large pitcher of dried hydrangeas. Photo courtesy of American Traditional Stencils.™

OPPOSITE RIGHT This beautifully executed floral design is the perfect accent for this posh and pretty window seat. The soft white walls brighten the room without seeming harsh. This relaxing retreat offers the perfect spot for powdering and pampering. Photographer: Eric Roth

FRUIT AND STRIPE DESIGN

A fruit motif is a classic design element that is still trendy today. The neutral colors in the striped background of this design translate beautifully into an understated and smart look. The stenciled fruit adds richness to the walls and complements any dining space or kitchen. Consider this technique for an entire wall, for a single wall, or for the space below or above a chair rail molding. Try painting the fruit motif on backsplash tiles or on cabinets, using the appropriate paint.

SUPPLIES

White latex paint
Neutral wall glaze
Pear stencil or stamp, 4¼" (10 cm) tall
Cherry stencil or stamp 3¾" (9 cm) tall
Small natural sea sponge
Large natural sea sponge
Stencil brushes, medium and small
Easy-release painter's tape (in two colors)
Measuring tape

ACRYLIC PAINT

Pale beige
Deep dusty rose
Dark flesh
Medium leaf green

Prepare or purchase all of the stencils. See Resources, page 124. Templates begin on page 114. Although this project was created with stencils, you can also stamp the patterns.

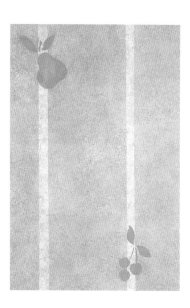

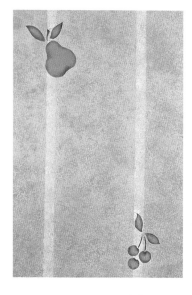

Step 1: Paint a basecoat of white latex paint on the walls. Mix equal parts of the pale beige acrylic or latex paint and the glaze. Use the large sponge, dampened with water, to sponge the glaze mixture onto the walls. Complete all of the walls with the sponged finish. The stripes in the featured project are 6" (15 cm) apart. Tape off the ³⁄₄" (2 cm) stripes using a pencil and a level. As you approach the corners, adjust the width between the stripes to ensure that a stripe does not end up in the corner. This adjustment makes the sponging process much easier. Using a mixture of white latex and neutral wall glaze, sponge on the stripes using the small sponge. Although you could paint on the stripes with a brush, sponging creates a softer, more textured look. Remove the tape as you complete each stripe.

Step 2: Next you will stencil the fruit. Place a small piece of painter's tape where you want to place each motif. Using two colors of tape allows you to indicate which motifs to place in which spot. The featured project shows the stenciled designs running along the stripes in a balanced design. After you have decided where to place all of the motifs, stencil them using the pale beige paint.

Step 3: Finally, you will use color to add depth to your designs. Stencil softly with the small stencil brush around the edges of all of the pears with the dark flesh paint. Repeat this process with the deep dusty rose paint around the edges of the cherries. Stencil around the edges of the leaves and stems of all of the motifs with the medium leaf green paint. If you are stamping, use appropriate colors for the fruit. Refer to the finished photograph for more details.

TUSCAN FRUIT VARIATION

This elegant variation is a stamped design of fruit and flowers. Apply the same background found in the Fruit and Stripes design, but do not apply the stripes. Cut a rectangle slightly larger than your stamps from stencil material. Randomly stencil these frames around the room with acrylic metallic copper paint. Make sure to use a small brush, and apply the paint only around the edges of the rectangle. See the photograph for more details. Stamp the fruit and flower design in the center of the frames. The beautiful stamps used in the sample are commercial stamps. Refer to Resources on page 124.

CLASSIC SCROLL BORDER

Elegant and architectural in style, the scroll border is an ageless approach to adding a formal embellishment to a living area, study, or foyer. The colors used in this project enhance the stateliness of the border. You can use this design in many different color themes. It would certainly be dramatic stenciled in gold on a burgundy wall, for example. The color grouping you choose determines the style of the design. Be creative and dramatic, and the results are sure to be dynamic!

SUPPLIES

Warm ivory latex paint

Neutral wall glaze

Classic scroll border stencil,
   14" long (36 cm) (one repeat)

Easy-release painter's tape

Stencil brushes, medium and small

Chip brushes

ACRYLIC PAINT

Sandstone

Copper

Burnt umber for color wash (optional)

Prepare or purchase all stencil templates. See Resources, page 124. Templates begin on page 114.

Step 1: Begin by painting your walls in an ivory latex paint. When applying glazes over a basecoat, you should use eggshell or satin finish for basecoat. If you are cutting your own stencil, cut two repeats of the same design. Beginning in a corner, stencil the border design in the acrylic sandstone shade. To avoid having to stencil around a corner, adjust the placement of the stencil so that you can end the design at the corner.

Step 2: Next, you will add shading and dimension to the stenciling. Imagine the scroll as a three-dimensional molding with a light source coming from above and a little to the left. Shadows would appear on the lower and right sides of each part of the design. These are the areas you will shade with the copper acrylic paint. Refer to the photographs for more details. Step back and see the results. Suddenly, the scroll stands out from the wall as if it were three-dimensional! If you would like to antique the walls, do a color wash of burnt umber and glaze or copper acrylic paint and glaze. Refer to Interesting and Easy Wall Finishes in Chapter 1 for color wash instructions (page 19). Before the wash is dry, soften the look by dry-brushing with a chip brush.

RIGHT This trompe l'oeil mural design conveys great tranquility. What a surprise to see this solitary bird perched in the window below the draped wrought-iron rod. The artist shaded and shadowed the elements in harmony with her light source. Notice it's subtle but significant role in the overall effect of the design. Photograph used with permission of Sheri Heoger, The Mad Stencilist.

OLD WORLD SCROLL BORDER VARIATION

This rich variation requires no shading of the stenciling. Use soft amethyst, rich soft green, and rose paint to stencil the design. When the paint is dry, softly sand over the design with 220-grit sandpaper. Refer to the photograph for details. Follow up with two color washes: the first of burnt sienna, the second of antique gold.

VIBRANT SCROLL VARIATION

Paint the upper wall in a soft yellow latex paint. Then paint the lower part of the wall in a rich green. Stencil the scroll design in yellow, 1" to 2" (3 to 5 cm) below the top of the green area. You can create this design in numerous color variations.

FLEUR-DE-LIS

Fleur-de-lis, which means "flower of the lily" in English, is a symbol that has existed for many centuries. This symbol represents a stylized lily or lotus flower and has many meanings. Traditionally, it has been used to represent French royalty and has embellished armor, banners, family crests, and other symbols of heraldry. It is unquestionably regal and powerful in its form and can stand alone as a splendid ornament or motif. It remains a design element that is often a component in sophisticated spaces.

SUPPLIES

Rich aqua latex paint
Chalk
Fleur-de-lis stencil or stamp,
  5³⁄₄" (15 cm) tall
Companion stencil or stamp,
  5¹⁄₂" (14 cm) tall
White acrylic paint
Stencil brushes, medium size
Craft sponges (if stamping)
Easy-release painter's tape
Measuring tape
Long level

Prepare or purchase all stencil templates. See Resources, page 124. Templates begin on page 114.

Step 1: Paint a basecoat on the walls using the aqua latex paint in a flat, eggshell or satin finish. You will apply the two motifs in the design in vertical lines, spaced 10" (25 cm) apart horizontally. Measure and mark your walls with chalk, allowing for starting or stopping points in the corners. Place an intermittent, vertical dash on the wall from ceiling to floor every 10" (25 cm). A retractable tape measure makes this process a bit easier. Be sure to use a long level to help keep your vertical lines straight. You can also use a plumb bob, which is made by attaching a small weight to the end of a string. After marking off the top of your walls every 10" (25 cm), tape the string to the mark and carefully make intermittent marks down the wall along the string. Check your marks with a long level. As you near a corner, adjust the vertical lines to ensure that the final stenciled line does not straddle a door molding or a corner angle.

Step 2: Go around the room, placing small pieces of tape where the motifs will be stenciled. The centers of the motifs in the featured project were placed every 16" (41 cm), vertically. The distance between your motifs depends upon the size of the wall or room and your preference. Stencil or stamp all of the fleur-de-lis (the larger design) motifs using the white acrylic paint. Follow up by stenciling or stamping the companion design throughout the room.

LAVENDER FLEUR-DE-LIS

This softer, more romantic version of the fleur-de-lis design begins with the wall technique called bagging or a form of frottage. Paint the walls in a light, dusty plum color. Make a glaze mixture by combining one part lavender latex or acrylic paint (slightly deeper shade than the wall color) to four parts neutral wall glaze. Follow the directions for the bagging and frottage technique found in Chapter 1. Let the walls dry. Randomly place painter's tape around the room to indicate where you want to place the motifs. Refer to the photograph for details. Using a soft purple acrylic paint, stencil or stamp the designs on the walls. The fleur-de-lis featured in the project has a contemporary, sleek twist. Either the traditional style or this contemporary style works well with this background.

NAVY BLUE VARIATION

This dramatic version of the design features only the crisp companion motif. Begin by painting a basecoat of navy blue latex paint. Then cut a 7" (18 cm) square from the stencil material. This square becomes the diamond for the border. The border, which is lovely at chair rail height, is made up of two shades of rich, bright blue. These colors are individually applied by pouncing the diamond stencil with a large sea sponge. Stencil or stamp the companion design at the horizontal points of the diamonds in metallic silver acrylic paint.

GOLD FLEUR-DE-LIS BORDER

Use this border at the top of the wall, at chair rail height, or above the baseboard. The small motif between the fleurs-de-lis is the center of the companion design. Paint a basecoat of golden straw latex paint. Then, stencil or stamp the motifs in ivory acrylic paint.

TUSCAN-STYLE FRUITED FLOWERPOTS

These stylish planters begin with standard terra-cotta flowerpots. Apply spackling compound to the pots and set them aside to dry. See the manufacturer's directions for drying times. When the spackling compound is dry, paint the pots with ivory acrylic paint. Brush on a mixture of equal parts beige acrylic paint and neutral glaze. Wipe off most of the glaze, leaving some in the crevices. Allow the glaze to dry. Apply a sponged white horizontal stripe, if desired. Stencil fruit using the same colors and method suggested for the walls.

FLOORCLOTH WITH SCROLL DESIGN

Floorcloths have been around for centuries. This lovely piece starts with a 3' x 4' (91 cm x 122 cm) piece of pre-primed canvas. Fold over a 2" (5 cm) hem, and adhere the hem to the unprimed side with double-sided carpet tape. Paint a basecoat on the primed side of the canvas with latex paint in light beige. Tape off a border of 1½" (4 cm), and fill in the border with a deeper beige acrylic paint. Stencil the scroll border on both short ends with beige paint. Finish by stenciling the long sides. Seal the cloth with several coats of a good quality water-based varnish.

FLEUR-DE-LIS CD BOX

Fabric-covered storage boxes are quite inexpensive and often devoid of decoration. Stenciling or stamping is a great way to embellish these organizers. It's a nice way to customize accessories to coordinate with your decor. The project accessory is a flip-top CD box. The acrylic paint used to stencil the box is a medium brown. Center the stencil over the lid. Stencil, concentrating on the edges of the cut-out design to place most of the color around the edges of the design.

Photographer: Bobbie Bush

*Elements of design that persist
through history deserve notice.
Their prolonged existence suggests
the promise of continued appeal.*

CHAPTER 4

CLASSIC DESIGN

This chapter features designs that are inspired by the art and elements of the past. Stenciling and stamping techniques have been in existence for thousands of years, but the materials we use to create designs today are quite different. Certainly the uses and styles have changed significantly as well. Many of today's patterns are reminiscent of the work of early itinerant artists who traveled the countryside of New England. The grace and simplicity of those designs are found in much of contemporary country decor. While the designs featured in this chapter are inspired by motifs from the past, the projects have a fresh approach to vintage ornamentation. The New England Leaf Design project, which was inspired by Moses Eaton's striking and colorful work, speaks for itself. Eaton is credited as being one of the most prolific itinerant artists in the New England area from 1800 to 1840. The Art Nouveau Calla Lily design is styled to resemble the remarkable and flamboyant patterns and art from 1890 to 1915. The Victorian Foliage project is reminiscent of leaf designs found between 1835 and 1905. The lush and ornate patterns associated with the Victorian period influenced this modified variation to suit today's style.

OPPOSITE LEFT This restful spot beckons the weary to pause and refresh. The natural woodwork lends warmth and a sense of antiquity to this space. Wide-planked wooden floors glow with a patina that upholds the sentiment of timeless endurance. The stenciled designs that decorate this space resonate the same simplicity and warmth as the surrounding elements. This ageless fruit and foliage theme does not detract from the sense of peace in the room, but celebrates it by adding its soft shades to the ivory walls above the plank-style paneling. Photographer: Brian Vanden Brink

OPPOSITE RIGHT This living area reverberates with color and style. The vibrant magenta of the loveseat receives added punch when placed in front of a rich blue wall. The juxtaposition of these colors works surprisingly well in the space. Soft yellow silk curtains add classic detail to the room. Stenciled vines crown the windows and cascade down around them, adding to the room's eclectic style. Photographer: Eric Roth/Zimman's

NEW ENGLAND LEAF DESIGN

This design is bold and graphic. It is especially beautiful rendered in the rich colors of the colonial period, but you can create it in any combination of shades. The featured project is designed for a divided wall. If you have a chair rail molding, you can apply the pattern below the chair rail. Without a chair rail, the pattern can solo by placing it an inch or two below the top of the green-painted section of the wall.

The addition of a stripe in this application, above and below the border design, is the perfect embellishment. The leaf design should be applied as a stencil when using it as a border design. The pattern is perfect for stamping if you will be applying randomly—as in our Shades of Brown variation—to create a more contemporary appearance.

SUPPLIES

Mustard gold latex paint
Deep, rich green latex paint
New England Leaf stencil, 17" (43 cm) long
Stencil brushes, small and medium
Artist's liner and flat brushes (optional)
Easy-release painter's tape
Level

ACRYLIC PAINT

Mustard gold

Prepare or purchase all stencil templates. Templates begin on page 114. See Resources, page 124.

TIP: A great way to add character and personality to a room is by adding moldings. Chair rail or crown molding (ceiling level) is easy to install if you have a miter box and saw. Home improvement stores carry many molding styles, as well as the directions to install them.

1

Step 1: If you have chair rail molding in your room, apply two coats of the gold latex paint above the chair rail. Then apply two layers of the green latex paint below the chair rail. If you do not have chair rail molding, create a horizontal line on each wall to mark the border between the gold and green paint. Make a mark every two feet around the room, measured 34" (86 cm) up from the floor. Join the marks with a pencil to indicate the dividing line between the top and bottom paint colors. Be sure to use a long level to ensure that your dividing line is straight. Paint two coats of the gold from the top of the walls to the line. Let the paint dry. Then place painter's tape just above the line and apply the green basecoat from the bottom of the wall to the tape. Once again, use the level to make sure your line is straight. Stencil the New England Leaf design 2" (5 cm) below the top of the green section of the wall. It is important to keep your design level and straight, however the design itself can be reversed to change the angle of the leaves. Refer to the photograph for details. Complete all of the stenciling in the room.

2

Step 2: If you do not have chair rail molding, this additional embellishment is optional. It adds definition to the border by creating lines above and below the stenciled design. Refer to the photograph for details. Mask off a ½" (1 cm) stripe just above the stenciled design and a ½" (1 cm) stripe just below the design. Paint two coats of the mustard gold paint and remove the tape. Use the artist's brush to touch up any imperfections.

IVORY AND GOLD NEW ENGLAND LEAF VARIATION

Place this border design at chair rail height, at the top of the wall, or anywhere in between. Begin by painting a basecoat of ivory latex paint. Refer to the photograph for details. Tape off a 5½" (14 cm)–wide border area wherever you will be placing the border design. This 5½" (14 cm) area will form the gold faux-painted border around the stenciling. The variation design was done using the bagging method, but you could also use a sponged finish. Use an antique gold latex (not metallic) or acrylic paint to tint the glaze. Stencil the design using ivory acrylic paint.

SHADES OF BROWN VARIATION

Paint a basecoat of soft cocoa. Tape off a 5" (13 cm)–wide border area, and paint between the taped lines using a deep toffee color. Refer to the photograph of this variation for the placement of motifs. Use a stencil or stamp to randomly apply the leaf designs using ivory acrylic paint. Some of the leaves will extend beyond the toffee border. Tape off 5" (13 cm) stripes above and below the toffee border. Paint two coats of ivory, creating horizontal stripes above and below the border design. Be careful not to paint stripes over the leaves that extend out from the border. Examine the border stripes in the photograph for details.

ART NOUVEAU CALLA LILY

The term *Art Nouveau* describes the "new" art that shaped the world of design just before and after the turn of the twentieth century. Although the free-flowing motifs of the period were generally based on nature, they were fresh and completely free of established design rules. The Calla Lily project exemplifies these principles. The raised design's crisp and curving lines are graceful yet dramatic when executed in this unique style. This procedure appears to be complex, but it is actually simple and straightforward. The spackling compound provides dimension to the motif and texture to the space.

Prepare or purchase all stencil templates. Templates begin on page 114. See Resources, page 124.

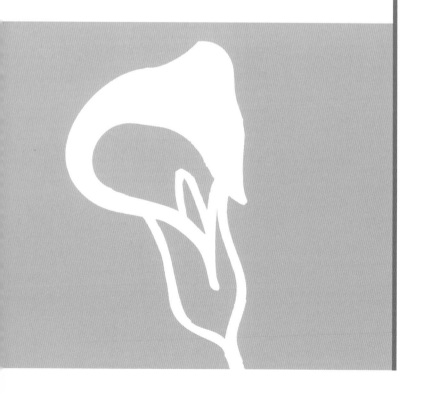

Step 1: Paint two coats of the blue-gray latex paint on the walls. Place small pieces of painter's tape on the walls to indicate where you will stencil the motifs. Apply the stencil adhesive to the back of the stencil. Place the stencil on the wall, and smooth it firmly to secure it in place. Carefully and evenly spread a layer of the joint compound over the cutout design and remove the stencil. Don't forget to frequently clean the joint compound residue from the stencil. Complete all applications of the motif throughout the room and allow the joint compound to dry. Gently sand the motifs and remove any dust.

① 1

Step 2: Place the clean stencil over the design. Dip your stencil brush in the medium blue acrylic paint. Offload most of the paint, just as you would when preparing to stencil any motif. Brush on the color in a circular motion. Complete this process on all raised designs in the room.

Step 3: Place the clean stencil over the design. Follow the same procedure as in step 2, but with a very small amount of silver paint. The goal is to highlight the design. Do not completely cover the blue motif. The finished raised design should have a silvery blue shimmer. Highlight all of the raised motifs in the room with the silver paint.

② 2

③ 3

CALLA LILY REPEAT VARIATION

This variation repeats the pattern to create the look of wallpaper. Paint a basecoat of warm blue-gray latex paint. Determine the placement of your motifs, depending upon the size of the wall or room and your preference. The motifs in the featured project are applied in vertical lines that are spaced 7" (18 cm) apart, horizontally. Make a plumb bob by attaching a small weight to the end of a string. After marking off the top of your walls every 7" (18 cm), tape the string where the first mark is and carefully make intermittent marks down the wall along the string. Check your marks with a long level. As you near a corner, adjust the spacing of the vertical lines to ensure that the final stenciled line does not overlap a door molding or a corner angle. Go around the room, placing small pieces of painter's tape to indicate where the designs will go. The centers of the motifs in the sample project were placed every 11" (28 cm), vertically. Using light blue-gray acrylic paint, stencil or stamp all of the calla lily motifs.

VICTORIAN FOLIAGE

This lush design was inspired by the decorative designs that adorned the parlors of the nineteenth century. Although its roots are from the Victorian era, the Victorian Foliage design merely whispers of those extravagantly ornamental days gone by. The leaves and berries that form the border and the coordinating single motif complement a variety of styles, from contemporary to traditional to retro. At the same time, its quiet personality flourishes in the company of other Victorian interior decoration. The featured variations illustrate this design's flexibility.

SUPPLIES

Soft green latex paint
Victorian Foliage Border stencil,
    17" (43 cm) long
Victorian Foliage single motif handmade
    stamp, 4" (10 cm) square (optional)
Pale moss green stencil paint
Small craft sponge
Medium stencil brush

Prepare or purchase all stencil templates. Templates begin on page 114. See Resources, page 124. If desired, prepare the single motif stamp.

Step 1: Paint a basecoat of soft green latex paint. Place small pieces of painter's tape to indicate where the designs will be stenciled or stamped. The sample project shows the border placed at the top of the wall, just below the ceiling level.

Step 2: Stencil the border design, continuing around the room until all of the walls are complete. You can also extend the design down (see photograph) in the corners or around windows and other moldings. The border pattern is designed so that the far left part of the design can be used as a single motif. Apply this single motif randomly on the walls. You can achieve this random placement with a stencil or handmade stamp.

(1)

(2)

VICTORIAN FOLIAGE WITH RED BERRIES VARIATION

This variation of the Victorian Foliage design, which brings the berries to life using a cranberry color, would complement any room, but is especially comfortable in these shades embellishing a colonial or country decor. Paint a basecoat of ivory latex paint. Stencil the green leaves, masking off the berries to protect them. Paint the berries in a lovely shade of berry red.

VICTORIAN FOLIAGE ON BURGUNDY WALLS VARIATION

This variation utilizes color as the Victorians did. The deep, dark burgundy walls create a dramatic canvas for the white stencils. The background combines the bagging technique with sponging. Begin by painting the walls in deep burgundy latex paint. You should plan to apply several coats for good coverage. Using the bagging technique, apply a glaze mixture of one part burgundy paint (slightly lighter than the wall paint) to four parts neutral wall glaze. For added drama, randomly sponge on a glaze mixture that is slightly lighter than the previous glaze. The secret to creating this subtle effect is to use glaze mixtures very close in color to the wall shade.

CALLA LILY TRAY

This wooden tray is both functional and decorative. Make a stamp of the calla lily using the template in the Patterns and Templates chapter. Seal the wood with an acrylic sealer. Apply two coats of deep, warm blue acrylic paint to the tray, and allow the paint to dry. Tape off a 10" x 6" (25 cm x 15 cm) border. Use a small sea sponge to pounce on one coat of silver acrylic paint. Do not apply too much paint. Refer to the picture for details. Apply the calla lily design using your homemade stamp. Apply three coats of water-based varnish to protect the finish.

CANDLE WITH NEW ENGLAND LEAF DESIGN

This is an inexpensive and simple way to create a coordinating accessory. Vanilla-scented candles are available at most department and discount stores. Stencil the New England Leaf design on the candle in acrylic paint. Many color combinations are suitable for the project, but if you are using the project design to decorate your room, simply use the same color combination on the candle. Tape the stencil on a large three-wick candle and stencil on the design using acrylic paint. Create depth and dimension by shading the design with a deeper shade of the same color. The sample candle was painted with two shades of leaf green.

VICTORIAN FOLIAGE MIRROR

Coordinating your home decor can be easy, economical, and fun. This charming mirror helps to create the impression of a custom interior. Purchase an unfinished mirror in a craft store. The sample project mirror has a removable panel that can be embellished to your liking. Tape off the mirror to protect it from paint. Paint two coats of ivory acrylic paint on the mirror frame and insert. Stencil or stamp the design in leaf green and berry red acrylic paint. Apply two coats of water-based varnish to protect it.

Photographer: Bobbie Bush

ABOVE This funky and vivid grouping is an exciting example of a popular style. The large cherry motif layered on the classic black-and-white diamond pattern has a stunning effect. This sassy approach to design blends whimsy with formality. Photographer: Keith Scott Morton

ABOVE TOP Primary colors really make a splash in this kids' room. The brilliantly colored borders make this aquatic theme truly dynamic. Stimulate the eye with bright, bold style as shown in this corner space. The bright yellow and blue used on the walls create a vivid palette for these sea creatures. Provide visual interest by constructing and embellishing a simple window cornice. These budget furnishings are truly transformed with a bit of imagination and a little paint. Photo courtesy of American Traditional Stencils.™

CHAPTER 5

WHIMSICAL SPACES

Every one of us has an imagination. It is the creative and playful part of us that transforms our practical knowledge into something infinitely more interesting and exciting. Imagination may remain dormant much of the time, but it is there. It manifests itself in some individuals as art. In others it seems to be applied logically. When decorating the home environment, push your imagination to the limits. There should be at least one space in every home that has an impulsive and whimsical flavor to it.

Your children's rooms do not have to be pink or blue. Choose an unexpected theme and color, such as lavender, golden yellow, or mint green. The Buggy Walls theme is colorful and graphic in nature. Bunny, Bunny is a great design for the nursery or a child's room, creating a caring and cozy space for your little one. Jazz It Up stirs up an aura of entertainment in your den or music room. The capricious and slightly retro style adds pizzazz to your walls and is bound to have an uplifting effect on anyone lucky enough to enter the room! All of the ideas in this chapter are meant to encourage an imaginative and playful approach to stencil design.

OPPOSITE BOTTOM RIGHT Casual furniture calls for interesting and unique wall design. The simple motif on this warm red wall offers the perfect accompaniment to this trendy space. The wall color creates a warm stage for the whimsical line-drawn fruit to dance upon. The effect is original and unusual. Photographer: Bick/Freundin

BUGGY WALLS

This bright and colorful design is certain to be a hit with your little entomologist. The playful nature theme creates an indoor "habitat" sure to make every little creature feel snug as a bug. This colorful design is shown in the sample project as a divided-wall project. The strié technique, which is used below the chair rail, gives the illusion of a grassy area. The upper wall area creates a space for several colorful and quirky bugs to buzz about and enjoy the flowers. If you have chair rail molding, the flower border can hover just above it. However, the border creates a wonderful transition without a chair rail molding at all. The project includes stenciling, stamping, and faux-painting techniques to achieve an easy and amusing mural effect.

SUPPLIES

Soft yellow latex paint
Medium green latex paint
Neutral wall glaze
Ladybug stencil, 8½" (22 cm) long
Butterfly stencil, 9" (23 cm) long
Dragonfly stencil, 9½" (24 cm) long
Bee stencil, 8" (20 cm) long
Commercial flower stamp
  (see Resources, page 124)
Whisk broom for strié technique
Stencil brushes, small and medium
Craft sponge
Artist's liner and flat brushes (optional)
Easy-release painter's tape

ACRYLIC PAINT

Deep green
Purple
Red
Black
Yellow-orange

Prepare or purchase stencils. See Resources, page 124. Templates begin on page 114. Dash lines on template indicate areas that need to be cut as a separate overlay.

TIP: Use a light touch when applying paint to a stamp. If you apply too much, the paint tends to blotch and make the stamp slide when you apply pressure. Practice stamping on another surface before working on your project.

Step 1: Apply two coats of the latex basecoat, above and below chair rail height. To create the strié technique, tape off the chair rail molding or the dividing line between the yellow upper wall and green lower wall, as well as the baseboard molding. Mix equal parts of glaze and deep green latex or acrylic paint. Brush or roll on the tinted glaze in three-foot-wide sections. Holding the whisk broom to the wall, brush a straight stroke from the upper taped line to the baseboard taped line. Continue this process around the entire room.

①

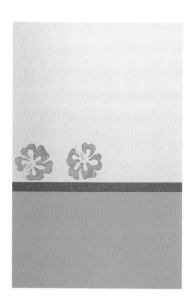

Step 2: Determine the spacing measurement between the flowers. For the sample project, we used 3" (8 cm)–spacing. Apply the yellow-orange paint to the stamen and two dots of the flower stamp using a small craft sponge or flat artist's brush. Immediately apply the purple paint to the petals. Apply the stamp above the chair rail height all around the room, reapplying the paint as needed.

②

Step 3: Determine how much space you want between each stenciled bug. For photography purposes, the project sample shows them placed quite close together, but you may wish to adjust them to a spacing that works with the size of your room. Go around the room placing a piece of painter's tape to indicate where each stencil should go. Write the name of the bug to be used on each piece of tape. Using a stencil mask to protect one cutout from another of a different color, begin the stenciling process. You should complete all of one type of bug in the room before proceeding to stencil the next type of bug. You can use an artist's liner brush to join the sections of the antennae of the bugs. Colors for the ladybug are red and black. The bee colors are yellow-orange, purple, and black. The bee's wings should be stenciled only on the outer edge of the cutouts to create a transparent appearance. Use purple for the wings of the butterfly, yellow-orange for the body, and black or purple for the antennae.

③

BUGGY WALLS WITH PURPLE PUNCH VARIATION

This variation calls for random placement of the bug motifs and stamped designs. Paint a basecoat on the walls with pale lavender latex paint. Sponge on a glaze mixture of one part light purple to two parts neutral wall glaze. If you'd like, you can sponge on a third glaze of one part medium purple to two parts glaze. Stencil the dragonfly using apple green, aqua, leaf green, and purple. The butterfly is stenciled using orange, pale peach, and soft yellow. See Resources, page 124.

BUNNY, BUNNY

This adorable assortment of fluffy stenciled bunnies is the perfect way to embellish the baby's room and will certainly be enjoyed for many years to come. The pictured color combination works for a boy or a girl, and can be customized any way you like. You might consider a sky blue background with white bunnies and deeper shades of orange and green for the carrots. Although the design uses the bunnies as a border at chair rail height, you can place them in many other locations. For example, try placing them at baseboard level in simple hand-painted tufts of grass, using the carrots to form a border. However you decide to use the designs, they're guaranteed to give your little one years of enjoyment.

SUPPLIES

Rich pastel green latex paint
3 Bunny stencils 6", 7½", and 8"
 (15 cm, 19 cm, and 20 cm)
Carrot stencil, 7" (18 cm)
Stencil brushes, small and medium
Flat artist's brush
Easy-release painter's tape

ACRYLIC PAINT

White
Heather
Bright peach

Prepare or purchase all stencils.
Templates begin on page 114.
See Resources, page 124.

T I P: When taping off long stripes, remember to use shorter lengths of tape. You will find that applying level stripes is much less difficult and the tape a lot easier to handle.

Step 1: Apply two coats of the latex basecoat in a rich pastel shade of green. Here, the first coat has been applied and the second coat is in progress. Let the paint dry thoroughly. For the white stripe, measure the wall 34" (86 cm) from the floor and mark lightly with a pencil. Continue marking this height all around the room. Apply painter's tape to the wall, leaving a ³⁄₈" (1 cm) stripe between the pieces of tape. Press the tape firmly on the inside edges, rubbing it down so that paint will not seep under the edges and create an uneven stripe. If this does occur, just take an artist's brush and repair the seepage with the basecoat color. With a flat artist's brush, paint two coats of white acrylic paint within the two strips of tape. Remove the tape immediately, before the second coat of paint dries.

Step 2: Tape off a ¼" (5 mm) stripe ¼" (5 mm) below the white stripe. Paint this stripe in the heather color. Begin stenciling the white bunnies just above the white stripe, as though they are sitting upon the stripe. Continue stenciling them around the room at intervals that appeal to you. The samples were done randomly about 3" to 4" (8 cm to 10 cm) apart.

Step 3: Now that the bunnies are done, tape off a ¼" (5 mm) stripe ¼" (5 mm) above the white stripe. This coral stripe is intermittently applied, between the bunnies. Using the bright peach and the heather paint, stencil the carrots randomly and at varying angles around the room above the bunny border. Flip the carrot over and stencil using the opposite side to vary the look of the carrot.

TIP: When painting a taped area, always remove the tape as soon as possible. Letting the paint dry increases the chance that the tape will strip off some of the new paint when you remove it.

BUNNY, BUNNY VARIATION

This endearing variation would make any toddler's room a friendly and inviting space. These little bunnies are cavorting up and down the hill. The fluffy fellows are stenciled in ivory and are placed on a deep rose background. Little stamped bees are buzzing about their ears as they play in the grass. Stencil the carrots randomly around the room, flipping the stencil over to create the reverse shape.

JAZZ IT UP

This stenciled and stamped design is a great way to jazz up any room. This fun motif works beautifully in your music room, family room, or on the wall near your piano. What a nice way to make practice time a bit more interesting. The featured design is rich in drama. The warm blue-gray background is an excellent canvas for the flamboyant stenciled instruments and stamped music notes. Placement of the elements is entirely up to you. Turn them into a border or splash them randomly on the wall in any color combination you please. Paint an apple green background and combine it with stenciled white instruments and deeper green notes for a crisp, contemporary look. Let the notes march around your wall or within a border. Why not use your existing white wall paint? Just stencil and stamp the motifs in primary colors. Use your imagination; these fun shapes demand it.

SUPPLIES
Rich blue-gray latex paint
Keyboard stencil 10½" (27 cm)
Saxophone stencil 8¾" (22.5 cm)
Handmade musical note stamps
Stencil brushes, small and medium
Artist's liner brush and flat brush
Easy-release painter's tape

ACRYLIC PAINT
Deep blue-gray
White
Black

Purchase or prepare all stencils.
See Resources, page 124. Templates begin on page 114.

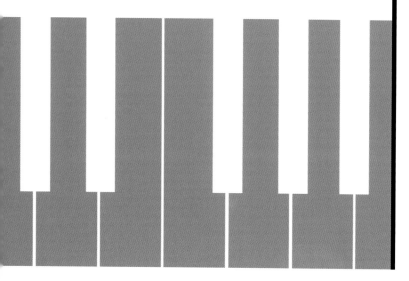

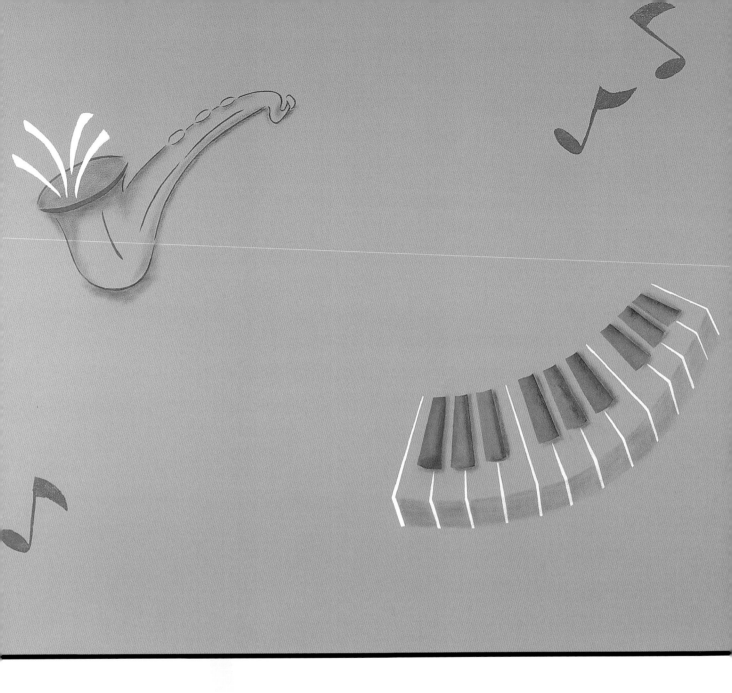

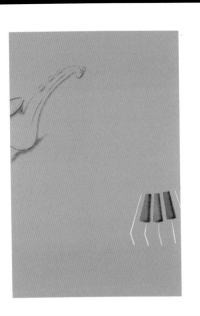

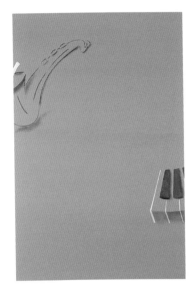

Step 1: Paint the walls with two coats of latex paint in the rich blue-gray shade. Decide how far apart you want to space the stencils, and place a piece of painter's tape to indicate where you will place the stencils. Begin by stenciling the keyboard. You will need to use a stencil mask when stenciling the black keys in order to protect the white key lines. Stencil the black keys using the blue-gray paint. Continue by stenciling the white detail lines of the main keys. Use the deep blue-gray paint to stencil the saxophone. Continue around the room until all of the instruments are stenciled. Sketch the two notes at full size. Prepare your handmade stamps (or stencils) and place them on the wall as desired.

Step 2: Next, you'll add dimension and depth to your stenciling by applying shading and shadowing. You can skip this step if you are pleased with the look you have at this point. Before continuing with this step, study the finished wall sample for placement and detail. To apply shadowing to the dark keys, place the stencil over the keys and slightly to the right, where the shadow should be. Softly brush on the black or gray stencil cream beside each key. Reposition the stencil to shade the front part of the black keys. Repeat the process for each key. Using the sample photo for detail, add shading and shadow detail to the front of the white piano keys and to the saxophone.

Step 3: Sketch the two notes at full size. Prepare your handmade stamps. Apply the deep blue-gray paint to the musical note stamps and randomly stamp the notes in pairs around the instruments. Use the artist's brush to touch up the notes where needed. If desired, use a flat artist's brush to paint the saxaphone's sound waves.

JAZZ IT UP VARIATION

This vibrant, animated variation of the Jazz It Up design begins with a white wall that has had a soft random ragging technique applied. The ragged-on glaze is one part dark flesh acrylic paint to two parts glaze. Then a color wash of one part burnt umber acrylic paint to two parts glaze is applied and worked thoroughly with a chip brush. The instruments are stenciled in red iron oxide and shaded with burgundy stencil cream or paint. The stamped musical notes marching across the wall are an unexpected surprise. Medium bright blue paint was used to give the notes their electric character.

ACCESSORIES

BUGGY STORAGE CUBE

You can use this unfinished storage cube, which was purchased at a local craft shop, to store baseballs and gloves, blocks, or all of those little stuffed animals scattered about the room. Paint the exterior of the cube with a soft yellow acrylic basecoat. Paint the interior in white or yellow acrylic paint. Tape off the edges of the cube, referring to the photograph for details. Paint the edge stripes in deep periwinkle blue. Coordinate the colors of the bug motifs with your wall stenciling. Seal the piece using acrylic varnish.

BUNNY, BUNNY BENCH

This unfinished bench with its flip-top seat is a great storage space for toys or seasonal clothes. Placed under a window, it is the perfect spot for daydreaming! Spray a basecoat of white satin latex aerosol paint on the sides and top panels. Paint the front and back panels in periwinkle blue. Following the stripe and stencil directions for the main project, apply the white and coral stripes and bunnies to the front of the bench. Apply the vertical carrots to the sides. The top can be finished in any way you please, using the carrot or bunnies in smaller sizes. Seal the piece using acrylic varnish.

JAZZ IT UP LAMP

This unfinished lamp is embellished with blue acrylic paint. The fabric on the shade is perfect for stenciling. Use the blue-gray paint to stencil the keyboard motif across the shade. Seal the wood with acrylic varnish.

JAZZ IT UP PILLOW

For a quick accessory, purchase a pillow at a local store. Pillows are available in a large variety of sizes, shapes, and colors. Just add a stenciled or stamped motif to customize the piece to coordinate with your room.

TIP: When stenciling on fabric, add textile medium to acrylic paint to help the paint seep more deeply into the fibers. Read the manufacturer's directions for more details.

CHAPTER 6

GLOBAL STYLE

You can bring the world a bit closer to home by incorporating meaningful symbols into your decor. Symbolism is the use of motifs and graphics to impart a meaning or message when words are insufficient. Symbols, which have been used around the world as decorative elements for centuries, are generally pictorial in nature and often beautiful in form. In essence, symbols represent words in the form of art. Some of the projects in this chapter incorporate historical and ethnic symbols. Some include stylized versions of symbols that are representative of a culture.

The Far East design features deep colors and dramatic motifs to create the aura of the Orient. The Song of Kokopelli is based on a centuries-old Native American legend. The hunchbacked figure is believed to symbolize fertility and the restless spirit. In the Native American project, Kokopelli is combined with other traditional and decorative symbols to create a warm and interesting wall design. African Adinkra symbols were first used in West Africa on hand-printed and embroidered cloths. The symbols used in the African Adinkra project represent man's essential attributes. Consider enriching your environment with cultural symbolism. Use traditional colors, or add interest by blending traditional shapes with a fresh color palette.

OPPOSITE This exotic and dramatic bedroom in British Colonial Style is full of color and texture. Behind the bed is a pair of stylized palm trees that extend up to unite with the beautiful border, just below a massive beam. The theme is repeated in the elephant pillows and stenciled zebra floorcloth. A container of proteas appears to be blooming on the bedside table to the left of the stenciled basket on the wall. The majesty created by the huge palms is the perfect setting for the impertinent little pug who never needs to be let out. The dark, rich furnishings complement the tone and scale of the room design. The shelf and accessories over the bed create a trompe l'oeil effect. All designs by Dee Keller of DEESIGNS, Ltd. Photographer: Barry Halkin.

THE FAR EAST

Bring the magic of the Orient into your home. These elegant stylized Asian motifs suggest the allure of the Far East. The featured project is rendered in classic reds and gold. The decorous opulence sets the mood for an eclectic arrangement of furnishings in the room. Rich-colored fabrics with luxurious textures would blend nicely with this dramatic setting.

The Eastern influence in design is punctuated with a sense of tranquility and peace. This impression of harmony and quietude in our environment is certainly in keeping with the desire for uncomplicated living spaces.

The motifs in the project are stenciled and stamped on the wall. The lower wall has been sponged and bordered with gold acrylic paint. For a softer look, color wash burnt umber over warm white walls. Stamp or stencil the motifs randomly in antique gold or charcoal.

SUPPLIES

Deep red latex paint
Metallic gold acrylic paint
Neutral wall glaze
Large natural sea sponge
Handmade square stamp,
  4¼" (10 cm) square
Far East Intertwined stencil,
  3" (8 cm) square
Far East Scroll stencil, 6¾" (17.5 cm) long
Small craft sponge
Stencil brush, medium
Artist's flat brush or small sponge brush
Easy-release painter's tape

Prepare or purchase all stencil templates. See Resources, page 124. Templates begin on page 114.

TIP: Choosing a wall color can be difficult. To get a specific wall color, play with acrylic paints, mixing them to the shade you want. Paint a poster board and try it in your room for a few days under various light conditions. When you have achieved the color you want, take the poster board to your paint store and have them match the color.

Step 1: Paint a basecoat of deep red latex paint on the walls. You will have to paint two or more coats to ensure full coverage. Mark a line around the room 34" (86 cm) up the wall from the floor. Tape off a ½" (1 cm) stripe on the line and paint it in metallic gold acrylic paint. Tape off the moldings to protect them from the glaze used in the sponging technique. Mix a glaze of equal parts metallic gold acrylic paint and neutral wall glaze. Using a slightly damp sea sponge, sponge on the glaze below the stripe all the way around the room.

Step 2: Use a small craft sponge to apply the gold paint to the square stamp. Stamp the square ½" (1 cm) above the gold stripe. Refer to the photograph for details. These gold squares will form a frame around the stencil. Stamp the gold square all around the room, just above the gold stripe. Using gold acrylic paint, stencil the design in the center of the square, using the photograph as a reference. After the border is complete, randomly stencil and stamp the motifs on the upper wall area.

BLUE AND GOLD FAR EAST VARIATION
(opposite page)

To create this lavish variation, you will use the bagging technique to produce a rich leather look. Begin by applying two or more coats of navy blue latex paint. Complete the wall by applying the bagging technique in a glaze of one part medium blue latex or acrylic paint to four parts neutral wall glaze. (See Interesting and Easy Wall Finishes in Chapter 1 for details.) After the glaze has dried, randomly stencil and stamp the motifs on the wall.

> T I P: For the sponging technique, use a grease resistant disposable plate for each color. Once you have paint on the sponge, pounce on a paper towel before applying paint to the wall. As the paint begins to set up, gently twist the sponge as you pounce. This softens the effect.

SONG OF KOKOPELLI

The legend of Kokopelli has existed in the Native American culture for centuries. The hunched-over, flute-playing figure was known as a storyteller and teacher, as well as the god of the harvest. His joyful and unrestrained nature was welcomed wherever he went. This inspiring figure is the center of this design. Other traditional Native American elements are used with the Kokopelli figure. Warm, neutral colors would reflect a rich, traditional palette. This project, however, was made with vivid colors to add interest to the motifs. Apply the design approximately 20" (51 cm) below ceiling level for an interesting look. To make a bold statement, make the patterns even larger than suggested.

SUPPLIES

Warm white latex paint
Neutral wall glaze
Kokopelli stencil, 5¾" (15 cm) tall
Deer stencils, 4¾" (12 cm) long
Bird stencil, 3¾" (10 cm) long
Sun stencil, 3¼" (8 cm)
Faux technique comb
Stencil brushes, small and medium
Small craft sponge
Chip brushes

ACRYLIC PAINT

Burnt umber
Teal
Soft burgundy
Soft brown
Mustard

Prepare or purchase all stencil and stamp templates. See Resources, page 124. Templates begin on page 114.

TIP: You can stencil most of the projects in this book using either type stenciling paint. Although a project may list acrylic paint for stenciling, feel free to use what you have on hand or prefer.

Step 1: Begin with a basecoat of warm white on the walls. Decide where you want the border to be, measure to that point, and tape off a 2" (5 cm) border area. Make a glaze of one part burnt umber to two parts neutral glaze. Apply the glaze mixture to the border area in manageable sections. Immediately use the rubber comb to create a wavy pattern in the glaze. Remove the tape from each section as you complete it. Create a wider border if your figures will be larger than the project size.

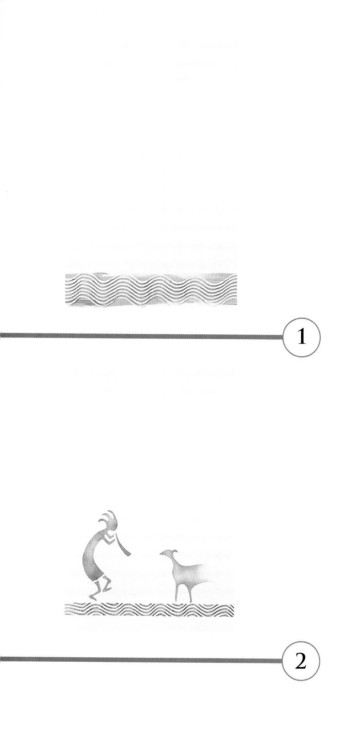

Step 2: Next, you will stencil the motifs just above the border design, making sure to clean the stencil and flip it over to vary the direction of the designs. Stencil the sun motif 10" to 12" (25 cm to 30 cm) above the Kokopelli figure using mustard acrylic paint. Repeat the motif, referring to the photograph for details. Continue stenciling around the room. Feel free to place the motifs as you like. If your motifs are larger than the project elements, space them accordingly. To create the bird's eye, just place a dot of paint on the face. You can apply a color wash of one part burnt umber, two parts water, and two parts glaze, if you wish. Work with a partner to brush on the glaze with a wide chip brush in large, sweeping motions. Working quickly, softly blot the walls with a slightly damp rolled-up rag. Follow up by softly smoothing out the harsher lines with a dry chip brush.

TIP: Many crafting tools can be handmade. Faux technique combs which are available in craft stores can be made from corrugated cardboard. Simply cut a square piece. Holding it at an angle, comb through the wet paint. Practice this process before attempting it on your project.

TERRA-COTTA VARIATION

Begin with a basecoat of light terra-cotta latex paint on the walls. Decide where you want to place your border, and tape off a 2" (5 cm) border stripe. Apply a glaze of one part burnt umber to two parts glaze to manageable sections of the border. Immediately after applying the glaze, use the rubber comb to create a wavy pattern in the glaze. Stencil the motifs in red iron oxide acrylic paint, just above the combed border stripe.

RANDOM MOTIF VARIATION

Paint the wall with off-white latex paint in an eggshell or satin finish. Randomly apply the stencils on the wall. The stencil colors used in this variation are the same as those in the main project. The coil design and small checkerboard design are commercial stamps. However, you can easily make your own stamps. Stamp the designs, referring to the photograph for details. Apply a color wash of burnt umber, using the same proportions as in the main project. This variation would be very interesting above a chair rail molding with a deep khaki paint below the molding.

AFRICAN ADINKRA

The fascinating motifs in this design originate with Adinkra cloth, which is hand-printed and hand-embroidered by the Ashanti of Ghana. Although originally used only by royalty and religious leaders during ceremonies, the symbols from Adinkra cloth now enjoy widespread use in clothing and other products. The numerous symbols contain messages in their patterns. The symbols used in the featured project were selected for their positive and powerful messages. The group located in the center of the photograph, from left to right, represent faithfulness and benevolence, unity in diversity, and bravery and valor. The color palette is vivid and upbeat to pay tribute to the courage of the Adinkra message. To tone down the color, apply a burnt umber color wash to antique the walls.

SUPPLIES

Warm white latex paint
Soft yellow latex paint
Neutral wall glaze
Large natural sea sponge
Adinkra stencils, average size
  4" (10 cm) square
Handmade houndstooth border stamp,
  8" (20 cm) long
Craft sponge
Stencil brushes, medium
Artist's flat brush or small sponge brush
Easy-release painter's tape

ACRYLIC PAINT

Blueberry
Mustard yellow
Deep burgundy
Warm white

Prepare or purchase all stencil and stamp templates. Templates begin on page 114. See Resources, page 124.

TIP: For a bold, textural appearance in stenciling, pounce the color on with a fine-textured sea sponge.

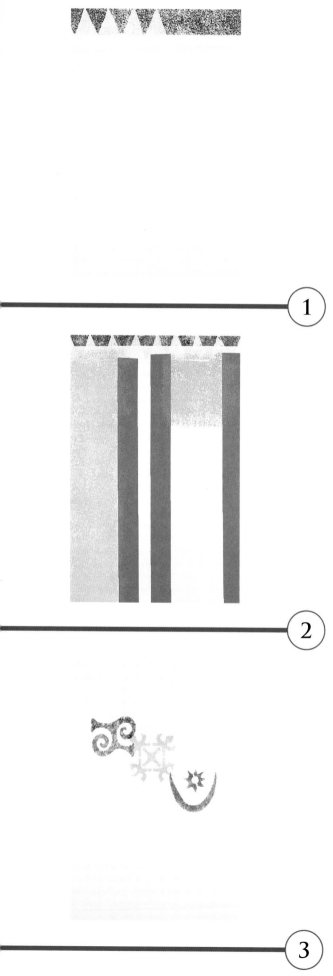

Step 1: Paint a basecoat on the walls in warm white latex paint. Mark a line around the room 34" (86 cm) from the floor. Tape off a 2" (5 cm) border stripe on the line. Prepare a glaze mixture of one part deep blue acrylic paint to four parts neutral wall glaze. Use a sea sponge to pounce on the blue border stripe. Make sure to remove the tape immediately. Create the houndstooth stamp using a 2" (5 cm)–tall triangle shape. Cut enough triangles to form an 8" (20 cm)–long border. Glue the triangles on a 2" x 8" (5 cm x 20 cm) foam-core backing, and let the glue dry. Use the craft sponge to apply warm white acrylic paint to the stamp, and stamp the houndstooth design in the blue border, all the way around the room. Allow the paint to dry.

Step 2: Using a pencil, very lightly mark 4" (10 cm) vertical stripes below the houndstooth design and tape them off. Don't forget to tape off the houndstooth border as well to protect it. Refer to the photograph for details. Mix a glaze of one part mustard acrylic paint to four parts glaze, and sponge on the glaze in every other stripe. Allow the glaze to dry.

Step 3: Using small bits of painter's tape, mark the areas where you want to place the Adinkra symbols. Remember to place the symbols in a random design. Stencil groups of symbols in burgundy, blueberry, and mustard yellow acrylic paint around the room. Refer to the photograph for details.

T I P: Anyone can stencil and the results can be satisfying. Artistry in stenciling requires going a step further. It involves adding detail by shading the design and by creating shadows. These additional embellishments add depth and dimension. Adding freehand strokes with paint can give the illusion of hand-painted artwork. You may not be an artist, but you can add artistry to your creations.

AFRICAN ADINKRA VARIATION

This lovely variation features the bagging technique along with the sponging method. Begin by painting a basecoat of warm white latex paint. Create a glaze using equal parts mustard latex or acrylic paint and neutral wall glaze. Apply the bagging technique to the walls using the mustard glaze. (See Interesting and Easy Wall Finishes in Chapter 1 for details). Mix another glaze using a slightly deeper mustard shade. Use a light touch to randomly sponge the deeper mustard glaze over the bagged finish, skipping some areas to create a textured effect. Stencil the designs in warm white. Using a fine artist's liner brush, accentuate the areas where shadowing would occur using a deep mustard color.

FAR EAST TABLE ACCESSORY

You can find beautiful place mats at discount department stores and home stores. The place mat used in this project is reversible. You can arrange your place settings on it or use it to grace an occasional table. The classic style will add elegance to any decor. Mix textile medium with gold acrylic paint, following the manufacturer's directions. Use a small craft sponge to pat the paint onto the square stamp. Then apply the stamp to the top left and lower right corners of the place mat. Add the stencil to the middle of the square. Repeat this process on the lower right side of place mat.

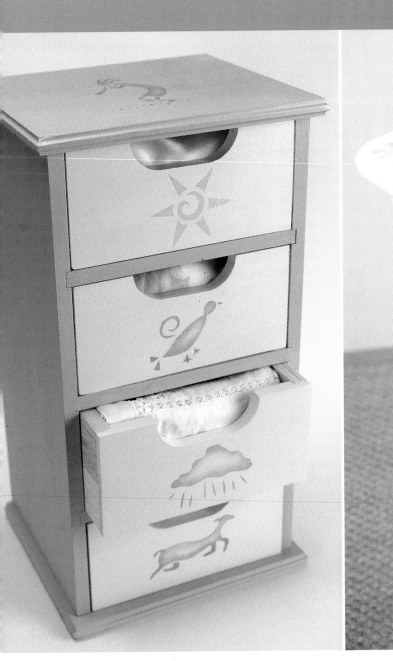

NATIVE AMERICAN CHEST

The wooden chest used in this accessory project is an unfinished pine piece. Begin by sanding the chest and removing the dust with a tack cloth. Paint two coats of warm taupe latex enamel on the cabinet. Refer to the photograph for details. Paint the drawers in two coats of light taupe latex enamel. Using burnt umber, mustard, and light blue stencil paint, apply the stencils as shown in the photograph. Finish the project by applying three coats of water-based varnish for protection.

Photographer: Bobbie Bush

AFRICAN ADINKRA TABLE

The table used in the project is an unfinished pine piece. Make a color wash by diluting taupe latex enamel paint with water. Using a sponge brush, apply the wash to the surface of the wood. Wipe off the excess glaze with a lint-free cloth. Find the center of the tabletop and mark it lightly with a pencil. Center the stencil over the pencil mark and tape it in place. Stencil the central design in soft green stencil cream. Stencil the four corner designs. Let the table dry. Apply three coats of water-based varnish, sanding between coats one and two.

GALLERY

ABOVE The stenciled laurel wreath and swag design on the linen accessories in this room offer the simple suggestion of elegance. The unusual light sconces create drama and add vibrancy to the rusty red walls. The overall effect is simple in its design, yet significant in its impact.
Photographer: Bick/Freundin

OPPOSITE A vibrant, tropical atmosphere is emphasized in this vintage bathroom. The original fixtures have been draped with an abundance of beautiful fabrics to exude an aura of grandeur. Even the walls are adorned with folds of fabric. The addition of bamboo accessories complements the theme. This basic bathroom has been transformed to a textural, sensuous space. The ferns and other plants can be painted freehand or stenciled and stamped. Photographer: Eric Roth

ABOVE This softly executed room mural is gentle in spirit. A mural such as this begins with soft color washed on the wall. Detail is added, layer by layer, using wonderful stenciled elements. The crooked sign nailed to the rustic fence begs to be personalized. The mood and depth of the mural is amazing. Photo courtesy of Stencil Ease International.

ABOVE This sweet and sentimental mural incorporates individual elements to create a serene atmosphere and sunny appearance in this fanciful nursery. Giant sunflowers, ferns, and lively birds adorn the sun-drenched walls of the room. Simple white furnishings and accessories complement the theme without competing with it. The white-painted wall shelf features real and stenciled objects for baby's viewing pleasure. The butterflies flutter about the room, as do the dragonflies. Photo courtesy of Plaid Enterprises, Inc.

OPPOSITE Odd furniture pieces with little in common suddenly coordinate and collaborate decoratively in a themed room such as this, simply by applying a coat of paint. This simple room with clean lines features colorful stencils with nautical style. The motifs are large and graphic and would work well in a den, study or boys bedroom. The theme is carried out in the accessories and the white-painted furnishings. Photo courtesy of Plaid Enterprises, Inc.

ABOVE This comfortable space is indicative of the casual lifestyle of today's homeowner. The gold wall, which is adorned by a single border motif placed at an unexpected level, makes an interesting and bold statement. The stark white of the stenciled design is an unusual and unexpected embellishment. Photographer: Bick/Freundin

ABOVE This room is an excellent example of adding visual impact by including a trompe l'oeil element on a stenciled wall. The stenciled limestone niche adds architectural interest to the rich reds. The exotic plant in the niche seems so realistic, one wonders if it needs a splash of water. Stencil designer Melanie Royals, Royal Design Studio.

ABOVE Color and pizzazz are the theme in this delightful bathroom. This fun renovation represents decorating on a budget at its best. These colors present an unusual combination but are delightfully warm and eclectic. The sink has been artfully draped to complement the beautiful stencil designs in the room and camouflage its drab shape. A "shabby chic" mirror and shelf adds a touch of rustic elegance to the room. The overall result is a wonderfully flamboyant ambience. Stencil designer Melanie Royals, Royal Design Studio.

OPPOSITE The flavor of the mysterious East is created here by Royal Design Studio. The exotic motifs and borders stenciled on the wall in soft, muted tones reflect an understated hint of Oriental influences. The table arrangement continues the mood with a striking Asian-style print, as well as unusual candles and a potted plant. The Eastern influence is beautifully portrayed in this setting. Stencil designer Melanie Royals, Royal Design Studio.

ABOVE This bedroom reflects a country French styling with rich raspberry walls. The space is full of surprises. A lovely stencil design has been applied above the bookcase and upon the sisal rug. The lounging dog and blazing fire are hand-painted dummy boards. Beautiful bed linens with matching valances and the upholstered chaise offer texture and comfort to the room. Upon close examination, you will find that the white bookcase is not furniture at all, but a painted illusion with stenciled objects and accessories adorning it. All designs by Dee Keller of DEESIGNS, Ltd. Photographer: Barry Halkin.

ABOVE Three little bunnies cavort in a garden in this wonderful mural. Stencil elements have been placed upon the blue sky background to create this wall art. This gentle scene is a lovely way to embellish a child's room or a sunporch and is sure to please all who view it. By Sheri Hoeger, The Mad Stencilist.

ABOVE This romantic English floorcloth combines an array of interesting motifs and patterns. The dynamic color combination is refreshing and unexpected. The borders are bold and formal while the center layout is delicate and lovely. The background of mottled greens bordered by lavender and pink adds a whimsical flavor to the ensemble. Stencil designer, Melanie Royals, Royal Design Studio.

BELOW How easy is this? A lovely vineyard growing just outside the window, and you didn't even have to put your spade in the ground! This mural will certainly fool the eye with its rolling fields in the distance. The absence of a cool, evening breeze is the only disadvantage of this trompe l'oeil window scene. By Sheri Hoeger, The Mad Stencilist.

ABOVE This farmyard mural is simply charming. The barnyard friends are certainly enjoying a beautiful summer day. The donkey, with his velvet nose just begs for attention while a pile of sweet pups stretch out nearby for an afternoon nap. These stenciled elements are so realistic you'll want to toss a little hay in the corner! Photo courtesy of Sheri Hoeger, The Mad Stencilist.

OPPOSITE Budget accessories can be embellished by stamping or stenciling them. This unusual lamp takes on new personality with the whimsical addition of the moon and stars. The little checkerboard border finishes the shade nicely. Photo courtesy of Plaid Enterprises, Inc.

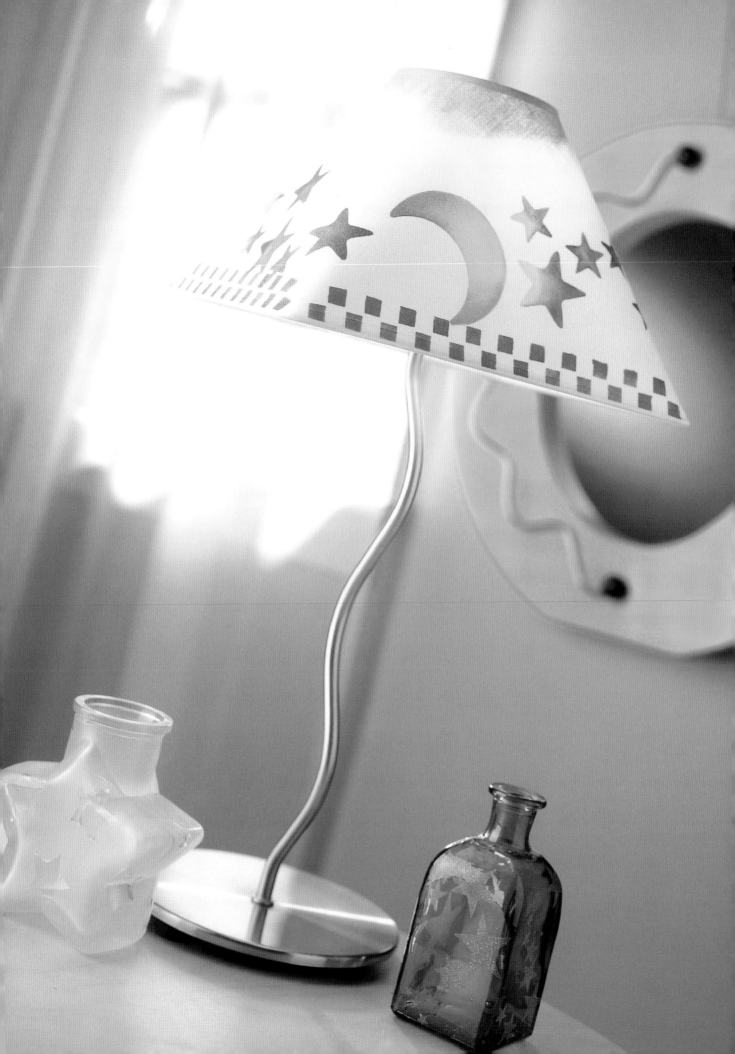

PATTERNS AND TEMPLATES
All percentages are approximate.

OCEAN BLUE, PAGE 22

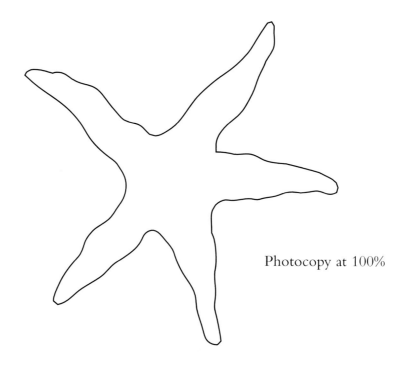

Photocopy at 100%

Photocopy at 150%

Photocopy at 185%

Photocopy at 154%

Photocopy at 100%

CLASSIC SCROLL BORDER, PAGE 42
Photocopy at 193%

FLEUR-DE-LIS, PAGE 46

Photocopy at 127%

ART NOUVEAU
CALLA LILLY,
PAGE 58

Photocopy at 140%

Photocopy at 150%

Photocopy at 174%

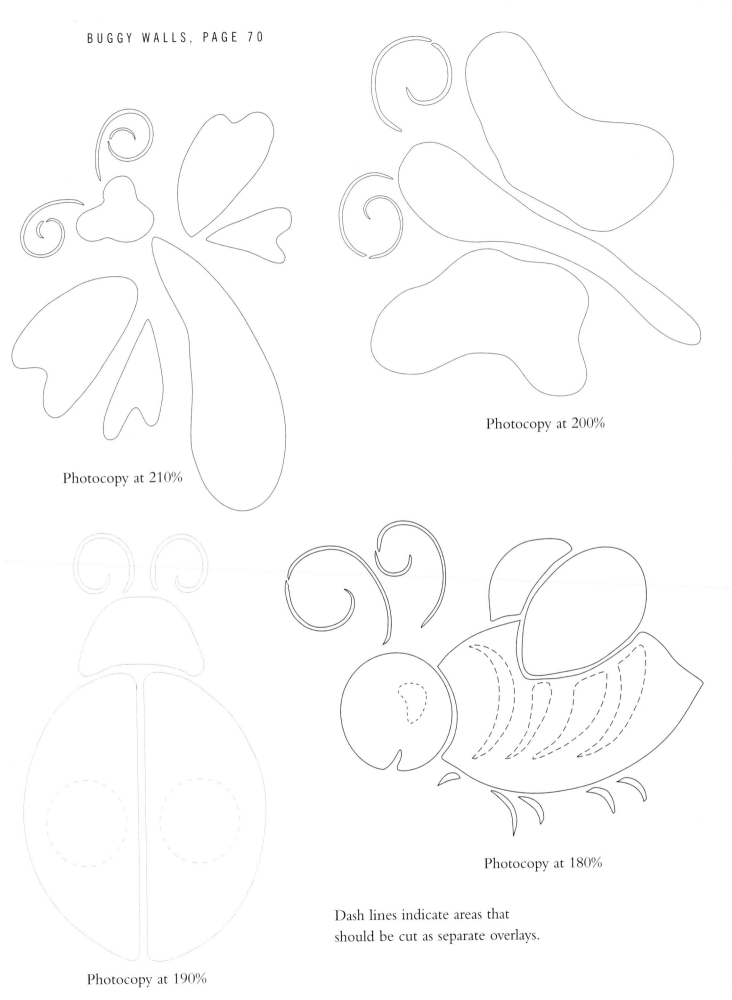

Photocopy at 210%

Photocopy at 200%

Photocopy at 190%

Photocopy at 180%

Dash lines indicate areas that
should be cut as separate overlays.

Photocopy at 150%

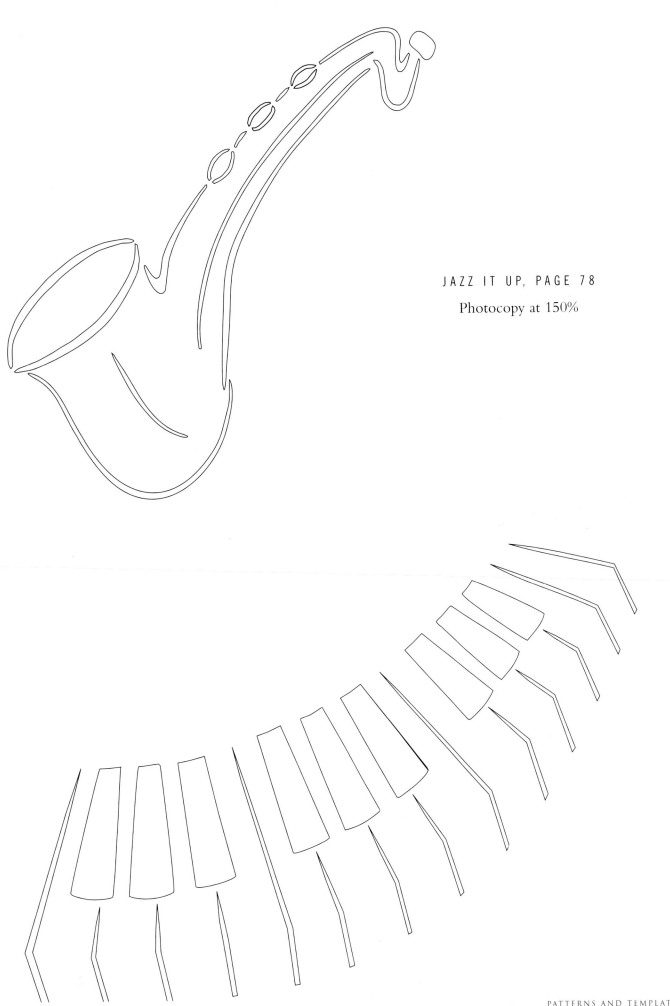

JAZZ IT UP, PAGE 78

Photocopy at 150%

FAR EAST, PAGE 86

Photocopy at 100%

Photocopy at 135%

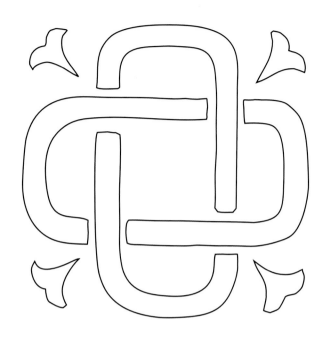

SONG OF KOKOPELLI, PAGE 90

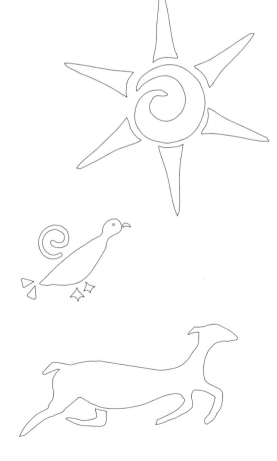

Photocopy at 190%

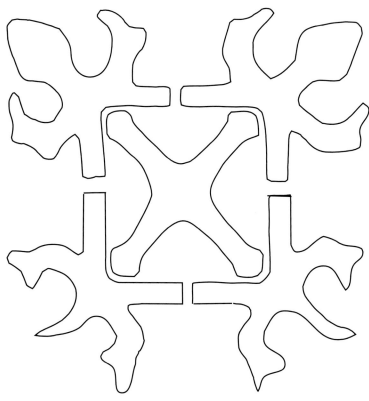

AFRICAN ADINKRA, PAGE 94

Photocopy at 100%

RESOURCES

Stencil Artistry by Glovier
332 Winter Quarters Drive
Pocomoke City, MD 21851
Phone: (410) 957-3987
Web site: www.stencilartistry.com
*Stamped and Stenciled Home patterns
and other designs in laser-cut stencils*

STENCILS, TOOLS, AND SUPPLIES

Bumble Bee Crafts
7 Toolara Street
The Gap QLD 4061, Australia
Phone: 07 3511 0068
E-mail: buzz@gil.com.au
General crafting supplies

Creative Art Stamps
399 Honour Avenue
Graceville QLD 4075, Australia
Phone: 07 3278 2814
General crafting supplies

Darice
13000 Darice Parkway, Park 82
Strongsvillle, OH 44149
Phone: (800) 321-1494
Fax: (440) 238-1680
Web site: www.darice.com
Foamies (foam sheets)

Delta Technical Coatings, Inc.
2550 Pellissier Place
Whittier, CA 90601-1505
Phone: (800) 423-4135
Web site: www.deltacrafts.com
*General supplies, acrylic paints, extender,
exterior/interior varnish, Stencil Magic,
Paint Creme, Top Coat Satin Spray*

Faux Effects, Inc.
Aqua Finishing Solution
Vero Beach, FL 32960
Web site: www.fauxfx.com
Aqua Glaze (neutral wall glaze)

HobbyCraft (stores nationwide)
Head Office
Bournemouth, United Kingdom
Phone: 01202 596100
General crafting supplies

Krylon
101 Prospect Avenue, N.W.
Cleveland, OH 44115
Phone: (800) 797-3332
Web site: www.krylon.com
*Home Decor Latex Aerosol used in
Bunny, Bunny project on page 74*

Loew-Cornell
563 Chestnut Avenue
Teaneck, NJ 07666
Web site: www.loew-cornell.com
*Stenciling and artist brushes used
throughout the book*

P.J. Tetreault
P.J.'s Decorative Stencils
P.O. Box 1212
Newburyport, MA 01950
Phone: (518) 330-5555
Web site: www.PJstencils.com
E.Z. Cut Plastic, stencil material

Plaid Enterprises, Inc.
3225 Westech Drive
Norcross, GA 30092-3500
Phone: (800) 842-4197
*Folk Art acrylic paint, Stencil Decor Gel,
Apple Barrel varnish, Folk Art textile
medium, storage cube on page 82*

Quilting Creations International
P.O. Box 512
Zoar, OH 44697
Phone: (330) 874-4741
Web site: www.quiltingcreations.com
Decorative Stencils by Doris Glovier

Rubber Stampede, Inc.
Phone: (562) 695-7969
Web site: www.rubberstampede.com
Extraordinary rubber stamps

The Stencil Shop
Phone: 44 (0) 1276 685429
Fax: 44 (0) 870 1209824
Email: Tracie@stencilshop.co.uk
Web site: www.stencilshop.co.uk
Offers a wide selection of stencils and paints

Walnut Hollow Woodcrafts
1409 State Road 23
Dodgeville, WI 53533
Phone: (800) 395-5995
Web site: www.walnuthollow.com
*Unfinished wooden items such as benches,
trays, and tables used in this book*

ORGANIZATIONS AND WEB SITES

Stencil Artistry by Glovier
Web site: www.stencilartistry.com
*Author Doris Glovier's Web site features
creative uses for stenciling and faux finishing
tips and ideas. Links available to many
other related sites.*

The Stencil Artisans League, Inc.
Web site: www.sali.org
*An international nonprofit organization
dedicated to the promotion and preservation
of the art of stenciling and related decorative
painting. Membership provides opportunities
for artistic and professional growth through
education, certification, public awareness,
and networking.*

**Martin Alan Hirsch Decorative
Finishes Studio**
Web site: www.fauxfinish.com
*The Faux and Mural Works Gallery features
beautiful works in all categories of faux and
decorative painting, including stenciling. The
site has an interesting and informative message
forum related to all areas of decorative painting.*

**The International Directory
of Decorative Painters**
Web site: www.fauxdirectory.com
*A Faux Finisher and Muralist Database
dedicated to listing and supporting talented
decorative painters, faux painting professionals,
and artists.*

CONTRIBUTORS

American Traditional Stencils™
442 First New Hampshire Turnpike
Northwood, NH 03261
Phone: (603) 942-8100
Fax: (603) 942-8919
Web site: www.AmericanTraditional.com
Blue Laser, brass and stainless stencils;
books and videos; tools and accessories; paints
Gold tone-on-tone room, page 36;
Fun Fish Room, page 68;
Woman stenciling, page 12

Susan Amons
Fancy Painters, Inc.
8 Heather Lane
Biddeford, ME 04005
Web site: www.fancypainters.com
Phone: (207) 283-6558
Seaside and Botanical Painted Floor, page 20

DEESIGNS Decorative Stencils
107 Jefferson Street
Newnan, GA 30263
Phone: (770) 253-6444
Fax: (770) 253-6466
Web site: www.deesigns.com
British Colonial Room, page 84;
Country French Style, page 109

Delta Technical Coatings, Inc.
Crafting and Art Supplies
2550 Pellissier Place
Whittier, CA 90601-1505
Phone: (800) 423-4135
Web site: www.deltacrafts.com
Whimsical bug patio set, page 6;
Lily of the Nile Room, page 14

Plaid Enterprises, Inc.
3225 Westech Drive
Norcross, GA 30092-3500
Phone: (800) 842-4197
Web site: www.plaidonline.com
Room with Stenciled Hydrangeas, page 10;
Apple Blossoms on yellow walls, page 17;
Fanciful, sunny nursery, page 103;
Nautical Room, page 104;
Moon and Stars lamp, page 113.

Royal Design Studio
2504 Transportation Avenue #H
National City, CA 91950
Phone: (800) 747-9767
Web site: www.royaldesignstudio.com
Extraordinary stencil collection; stenciling
tools and materials; books and videos;
Limestone Niche, page 106;
Parisian Urn Panel, page 14;
Romantic English floorcloth, page 111;
Whimsical bath, page 107;
East Meets West, page 108

Rubber Stampede, Inc.
Extraordinary Rubber Stamp
2550 Pellissier Place
Whittier, CA 90601-1505
Phone: (562) 695-7969
Web site: www.rubberstampede.com
Buggy Walls project (flower stamp), page 70;
Essence of Autumn project and Summer Leaf
Variation (leaf stamps), pages 27 and 29;
Tuscan Fruit Variation (fruit stamps) page 41

Stencil Ease, International
P.O. Box 1127
Old Saybrook, CT 06475
Phone: (800) 334-1776 or (860) 395-0150
Fax: 860-395-0166
Web site: www.stencilease.com
Home decorating stencils, stencil paints,
stencil brushes, and stenciling accessories;
Peaceful Valley Mural, page 102

The Mad Stencilist
P.O. Box 5497
El Dorado Hills, CA 95762
Phone: (888) 882-6232
Web site: www.madstencilist.com
Embellishment stencils, custom
lettering stencils, brushes, paints,
airbrush equipment, books;
Vineyard Mural, page 111;
Garden Grow Mural, page 110;
Bird in Window with checkered
valance, page 44;
Farmyard Mural, page 112

DEDICATION

To my family and friends. To my husband, George, who
believes in me and whose love I have been blessed to
experience for over three decades. To my parents, Pete
and Helen Cast, who are my biggest champions and have
been a huge source of encouragement and advice. They
are never too busy to listen and always rejoice in my
accomplishments. To my Mammy, Isabelle Leach, who is
a journalist and author, an inspiration in every way, and
my kindred spirit. Her enthusiasm and support during
the writing of this book meant so much! To all my friends
who have teased me and lovingly encouraged me, especially
Bill and Elaine Herz, who have believed in my creative
spirit and urged me to explore it. I thank all of them and
know that I am a very blessed person to have them in my
life. To my beautiful children, Jason and Emily. I love you
guys and thank God every day for sending you to me.

ACKNOWLEDGMENTS

I would like to thank the following artists and designers who generously contributed images of their own wonderful artwork or the designs and talents of their company:

Susan Amons, Fancy Painters, Inc.
Judith Barker-Joyce and Barbara Swanson, of
  American Traditional Stencils
Dee Keller, DEESIGNS, Ltd.
Melanie Royals, Royal Design Studio
Brian Greenho, Jeannie Serpa, Stencil Ease
Sheri Hoeger, The Mad Stencilist

Many thanks go to my friend and studio assistant on this project, Shirley Mason, for her enthusiasm and creative input. We had a blast together. I am so grateful for my husband George, who helped pack the endless shipments and who quietly and patiently assisted wherever and whenever he could, which was often!

I greatly appreciate everyone at Rockport Publishers for their guidance and assistance, especially Mary Ann Hall and Livia McRee, who made me stretch and learn and see things from a different perspective. Thanks to the art department and the photography department. They are all geniuses at what they do. A special thank you to Winnie Prentiss, publisher of Rockport, for helping me to reach an important goal — to write and create! I can't imagine anything better.

ABOUT THE AUTHOR

Designer Doris Glovier has a thirty-year history in arts and crafts. Her designs include all types of craft projects. Special interests include writing, drawing and illustrating, stenciling, and decorative painting, especially in relation to home decor. She has a stencil collection currently being marketed by Quilting Creations International, www.quiltingcreations.com, and is developing artistic designs for her new collection, Stencil Artistry by Glovier, www.stencilartistry.com. Many of the designs in this book are included in this collection. Doris teaches for a major craft store chain.